My Sweety

The Heartache of Loving a Deer

By Karen R. Hurd

**WESTERN REFLECTIONS
PUBLISHING COMPANY®**
Lake City, CO

ISBN 978-1-932738-99-5

Cover Art: Karen Hurd
Cover and Text Design: APH creative design

First Edition
Printed in the USA

Western Reflections Publishing Co.
951 N. Highway 149
P.O. Box 1149
Lake City, CO 81235
(970) 944-0110
www.westernreflectionspublishing.com
publisher@westernreflectionspublishing.com

Dedication

I dedicate this book to my husband, Robert. Robert, you helped me so much to take care of Sweety. I know there were times I put Sweety first and you tried to understand. I love you and thank you so much.

Jen, Lane, and Shaylee, thanks for putting up with mom's and grandma's obsession with Sweety. You're my sunshine! I love you with all my heart.

To Phil Mason, I couldn't have been with Sweety without you. Thank you for allowing me to have this wonderful experience. I still see you shake your head at me and laugh as you walked away. I pray that Sweety is with you up in heaven and that you are watching over him. He couldn't be in better hands.

To Don Cardin, what would I have done without your friendship, common sense, and honesty! I know you live to hunt, and yet you did all you could to make sure Sweety was never killed by a hunter.

Table of Contents

Sweety
1994 to 2005

INTRODUCTION

For years I have wanted to write Sweety's story and tell the world how wonderful he was. And, so, during the winter of 2009, I finally put what was in my heart on paper. I learned so much from this animal and will treasure every memory we shared together. I hope Sweety's story touches everyone who reads it in some special way. Maybe just by slowing down as you pass deer on the side of the roads, just to look at them or to prevent you from hitting one.

When the winters get so harsh and you begin to worry that the wildlife will pay a tragic price, maybe you might try and see if something can be done to help them survive. If this book can save one deer, then Sweety and I have done what we set out to do.

There are some things I know I will never put myself through again, as the heartache was sometimes too much for me to take. As wonderful as it was to know and love Sweety, it was also very painful.

CHAPTER 1

Our Yard

The yard looked like a hay meadow; field mice were everywhere. We were sure it hadn't been mowed or watered all summer long. The grass was completely brown and at least two feet tall. Yet, with a little imagination and lots of blood, sweat, and tears, my husband and I knew we could turn that hay meadow into one of the prettiest yards in Lake City. The yard was surrounded by moss rock and other rocks of all sizes. Chipmunks and squirrels had their own little paradise. The birds were abundant and sang so loudly we could almost dance to the music they made. Two marmots sat on a tall rock squeaking and watching our every move. We almost had our own private zoo. Having a daughter who loved animals as much as I did, this yard was going to be wonderful. The house wasn't real big, but large enough for the three of us, and a mansion compared to where we had been living. This was going to be the perfect place to raise Jennifer. My husband's biggest concern was that we were about two hundred yards from the cemetery, and he knew most of my family were buried there. He thought it would be hard on me, living so close to all of their graves. At first it was hard, but after taking several walks through the cemetery I began to find comfort in it, and it no longer bothered me.

We were completely moved in by August, and the yard already looked a hundred percent better. We mowed and watered it, and it was turning a pretty dark green, although it still needed more grass seed, as there were bare spots. We would fix that, but it just might have to be in the summers that followed. While we worked, our daughter Jennifer drove around on the small little child's four-wheeler we had bought her. The yard was so big that she would spend hours going back and forth. One day while we were out working, our dog, a Rottweiler we had named Bronc, started barking and growling like crazy. We had never heard him or seen him act like this before. We looked and looked in the area he was barking, and finally we spotted branches moving in a large pine tree at the east side of our yard. There, high up in the tree, was a mama bear and her two cubs. This was exciting. We knew there were bears around, but we had never had them in our own yard. It would become a common sight until the snow fell and the bears hibernated in the winter. We had a lot to get used to; getting used to bears was a real experience. I went weak in the knees a few times when they would come close to the house and look through our windows, but we soon learned that jumping up and down, clapping, or making a loud noise would send them off running in the other direction.

Bears visited our yard regularly.

Marmots lived in the rocks that surrounded our yard.

CHAPTER 2

Family

Robert and I married in 1975. I had started dating him when I was fifteen years old, and we married the day after my eighteenth birthday. He'd been working for the Hinsdale County Road Department and in 1983 became the road supervisor. We had our daughter Jennifer Dawn in 1979. In 1984, I began working for the United States Postal Service as a clerk. I'd lived in Lake City most all my life. My grandparents, Stella and Mike Pavich, ran the local grocery store and liquor store. They were my father's parents. We were raised mostly by Stella, though instead of calling her Stella we nicknamed her Mammy. Grandpa Mike died early in my life, and I don't remember him all that well. My mother's parents, Mick and Frank Mendenhall, also had a huge part in raising us kids, and I bonded more with them. We had nicknames for them, which were Moma

Mick and Daddy Frank. I was three years old when my mom and dad split up. I had two sisters and one brother, Linda, Cindy, and Steve. I was the baby. Our mom and dad had a lot of personal problems, alcohol being the main one, which pretty much forced our grandparents to take care of us. By the time I was twelve I had lost my sister Cindy in a car accident in which alcohol was involved. My father died in a car accident when I was seventeen. Again alcohol was the reason. And, when I was twenty-one, my mother died from an alcohol binge. So needless to say, I very seldom have a drink of alcohol. My mom once shot herself, luckily missing her heart. My father was stabbed right in front of us kids by his older brother who was drunk. My father was stabbed three times, barely missing his heart. He survived. Mammy also was stabbed in her face that day trying to protect my dad. Growing up in this atmosphere was such a learning experience.

My dad and I had problems early on in life, and we were never able to solve them. I found out after my sister Cindy's death the reason behind our problems – he thought that I wasn't his. I could never bring myself to ask my father if the rumors were true. My father's new wife confirmed the rumors once, yet I never found the courage to discuss them with my dad. God blessed me with a gift and that gift was I could draw and paint. My dad was a fantastic artist. I believe that God blessed me with this talent to answer a question that would haunt me the rest of my life.

My husband's parents also had been raised around the Lake City area. He had a huge family, five brothers and three sisters. I loved being with all his family; it was a family like I'd never known. They never had much money, but they all worked together and took care of each other. I heard stories of the kids going without shoes and so many other things that we take for granted. His mother was my husband's rock; she was the world to Robert. Robert's father died not long after we were married, but we were fortunate enough to have his mom around for several more years. Our daughter Jennifer was blessed to have a chance to know and love her. Charlotte was a huge influence on my daughter's life also. Charlotte was a huge influence in my life. I learned how to cook from Charlotte, and many more things that were important to insure that her son was taken care of. Charlotte lived long enough to see us move into our new home. She often rode the small four-wheeler of Jennifer's around in our yard. She left us with many valuable lessons.

Robert's mother Charlotte and Jennifer loved driving the 4-wheeler in our yard.

When I look back at my childhood, some of my fondest memories are of the animals I grew up with. While the world seemed crazy, I always found comfort with my pets. I had dogs, cats, rabbits, pigeons, and a horse. Animals put a smile on my face.

I'm hoping a little family history can explain my strong connection to animals. It seems all my life, when things weren't good or there was unhappiness, I would find comfort in a puppy, kitty, frogs, salamanders, horses; anything that had fur or feathers seemed to make me forget all the troubles mom and dad had, and kept a smile on my face. We'd gone through some tough times; and though I had many friends, my pets were the ones that never expected anything from me except my love. They, in return, always gave that love back.

Robert and his mother, Charlotte.

Lake San Cristobal in winter.

CHAPTER 3

Riverside's Mule Deer

Lake City winters are long and hard, as are most Colorado winters. It seemed that from September to May we did nothing but shovel snow, and we were always so ready for summer. Warm temperatures and green grass were very welcome. We liked winter – the snowmobiling, skiing, skating, and other winter sports were great fun – but there was always the worry of traveling. Slick roads were a constant worry. To see a doctor or get groceries or just about anything we might need, we had to travel to the next town, which was fifty miles away.

Since we lived about a mile from town, it was common to have deer, elk, coyotes, and bobcats running through our yard. We had several neighbors, but at that time not a whole lot of people had moved into the area where we lived. It was a common sight to see both bird and deer feeding stations in other yards. Back then, the feeding of wildlife wasn't against the law; or, if it was, it wasn't enforced. Lake City had a wonderful wildlife officer who realized the need for extra food for the deer and elk in the hard winters. He did say he never wanted a person to feed the animals to draw the deer or elk in to be killed for hunting purposes (which is legal in some states). He often visited my yard, and several times he witnessed my having an injured wild bird or injured rabbit in a cage. He would shake his head and say something like "you know Karen, you're not supposed to be doing that." And he would laugh and walk away.

Phil Mason was our local game warden. I've heard people say he didn't enforce some laws, but I feel (and this is my own personal feelings) that Phil knew how hard our winters could be. He also, I believe, knew that if several people threw out feed, the deer and elk would not congregate in groups, sickness wouldn't spread, and the animals wouldn't starve. Phil never tried to stop us or make us feel we were all doing something wrong or illegal, but when food was plentiful he did not want us feeding and we would stop. The only feeding we did was when we knew the snow was too deep and the loss of animals was going to be great. Phil did ask my husband once not to feed deer pellets, as he didn't want us just trying to attract the deer. We promised him we never would. He also came to me on several different occasions and asked about how the deer were, if there were many fawns, and how did they seem to be surviving the winter. Phil, in my eyes, was a great man. His love for animals, his concern, and his common sense knowledge that when there's four feet of snow on the ground animals were going to die, proved that point. He wasn't as strict as the Division of Wildlife wardens are today. Life has changed so much and the laws are so harsh. Phil being the way he was is the reason I'm writing this book. If Phil would have enforced the laws like they are required to do today, I would have never known and loved a beautiful mule deer I named Sweety.

Riverside Bucks Painting by Karen Hurd.

CHAPTER 4

The Riverside Bucks

The entire town of Lake City talked about the Riverside Estates mule deer bucks. They were absolutely awesome. There were about fourteen bucks that would be considered trophies to any hunter. These animals didn't get to this magnificent size by being stupid. We wouldn't see any of the deer until fall, when men in orange hats and vests invaded their high country. They must have known that shooting in housing areas was illegal and they could find safety there. Food was still plentiful in the high country, yet these deer knew they needed to come down. Over the years we got to know who was who, and the whole neighborhood had special names for each deer.

King was an absolutely beautiful buck. He had the widest spread; his antlers must have been 35 or 36 inches wide. He was something to see, so very, very, impressive. Every buck in the area respected King. King was short and stocky, but those antlers showed up a mile away. From a distance you knew exactly whose head they were on. We had the pleasure of watching him for years and waited and prayed each fall that he would show up to visit our yard again. I believe it was November of 2000, the day after Thanksgiving, King disappeared. That spring a local man, a hunter and friend Don Cardin, came to where I worked at the Lake City Post

King

Office to show me a skull he had found up in the mountains on the property he watched over. A sad day — I knew the minute I saw those huge antlers that they belonged to King. I was heartbroken, but glad it was Don who had found him. I knew Don would proudly display King to the world at the ranch where King grew up.

Prince

Prince was our second biggest mule deer buck. He was a 5 by 7 (five points on one side and seven on the other), with antlers that forked at the top. A traffic stopper; he too was beautiful. We heard Prince was illegally shot and killed in our upper Cemetery (little Lake City has two graveyards). I never grew too attached to Prince but enjoyed seeing him. I hated he had been killed illegally, and in our local graveyard – of all places to hunt! There was Handsome, Toughy, Beauty, Beau or Bo, Pretty Boy, Buster, Crooked Horn, Star, Magraw, Trouble, Squirt, and Bruiser; oh, we had quite a few, and each had something special. Riverside Estates was blessed with these magnificent animals roaming the area.

Bruiser

Bruiser was the first mule deer I ever got attached to. He was the first I ever petted or hand fed. He'd been in the area for years and was easy to recognize with his sword-like horns. He was just three points on each side, and some years only two points on each antler; yet both were long and wide. Bruiser was one tough old man. Maybe not a trophy in a hunter's eyes; but let me tell you there was not one buck in the Riverside area that didn't respect Bruiser. Bruiser was total attitude, completely and utterly full of himself. He bluffed his way through life and lived a long and full life by bullying everyone around. I will never forget the day my husband and I witnessed Bruiser take on a much larger buck we named Bo in our yard. Robert and I followed the two and watched as Bruiser made loud snorting sounds and thrashed his head about. Bruiser had Bo running with his tail between his legs. He was something else.

Dempsey

Bo

We experienced and learned many things. Mule deer are very intelligent animals. Mule deer care for each other and respect each other. The lessons we learned are valuable lessons. Growing up, deer meant food on the table. Today I feel differently. I'm not against hunting in any way, though I myself will never eat deer meat again. Some of my best friends were these four-legged creatures.

Squirt

ud Muffin

As Bruiser aged he taught us much about the nature and life cycle of a mule deer. His once sword-like antlers declined dramatically toward the end of his life. You could feel his sadness over the loss of his powerful antlers. He would hang his once-proud head down. That head, thrashing and snorting, had once made cowards among the others. Now Bruiser kept a safe distance away from the younger, much stronger bucks. It was sad to see, but we learned from watching him. His teeth nearly disappeared, and I even ground his food to try to keep him alive. Bitterly cold temperatures set in and the snow grew deeper. It was twenty below the morning we found Bruiser's eaten body laying in the snow. In one night, the coyotes had eaten all but his head. I didn't take his death well. I spent that day crying, throwing up, and lying in bed. I should have learned then not to fall in love with a wild animal. For awhile, during Bruisers life, I was unaware that I was getting attached to another young deer. My life would be changed forever by knowing and loving my new little friend. But to properly tell his story, I first need to tell the story of the others.

It is hard to understand how my husband and I got this involved in the lives of our local deer. We both came from families that hunted deer and elk to keep us fed. My husband Robert was an avid hunter and lived for October when he could head out to kill an elk or deer. I had cut up more venison than most women I knew. It was a way of life, and the last thing we wanted was to get attached. They were food, and they didn't have feelings, did they? Surely they didn't have individual personalities – or did they?

Toughy and Handsome. These two were always together.

One story that really got to me and my husband, and which proved how mule deer cared for each other, was the story about two bucks we named Handsome and Toughy. These two were always together, they were never apart, and if you saw one you could bet money the other was going to be there also. I got to know Don Cardin over the years because most of the deer we knew lived on the land he watched over for most of their lives. Don and I talked back and forth on who was who and he knew his animals as well as Robert and I. We connected well, and it was always fun to talk with him about the deer that were touching our lives. One day Don walked in where I worked, said a buck had been hit by a car, and asked me to drive out and see if I knew who it was. I headed right out after work, and as I approached the area where Don told me to go, I saw another buck standing close to the bloody and broken body of another mule deer buck lying off to the side of the road. There Handsome stood. I knew without looking who had been hit, it was Toughy.

I told Don and another man to watch and see if Handsome was still there, standing by his friend. Don's reaction was that the last thing he wanted to see was affection between these animals. It meant they had emotions. Don was an avid hunter. Don lived to hunt. He ate, drank, and breathed hunting. For two weeks, Don, Charlie Colopy, Robert, and I witnessed Handsome staying close by his lifeless friend. Don did not welcome this scene, it was sad to see. It was also the first time I had seen this behavior. I hated it. Finally, Handsome moved on. We all wondered if the two were brothers, or just friends. It was apparent that they cared for one another. I believe we all walked away with more respect for mule deer than we had before. As the winter months passed I saw Handsome many times. Handsome had found another friend, Squirt. I was glad to see that he wasn't alone.

I'd like to share one more story of animal connections before I go in to the main tale. This one though is not about mule deer. This is a true story about two cow elk that spent two winters together side by side until one passed away. Elk do not come to town unless they cannot survive in the mountains. Elk are proud creatures; and to get a good photograph, you usually need to be in Rocky Mountain National Park where they are used to people. Otherwise, the minute they sense you are there, they aren't. I love to paint and elk are one of my favorite animals to paint, yet getting good photographs has always been difficult . . . but let's go back to the two cow elk.

o old grandmas.

It was in the summer when we noticed the two hanging around the Riverside Estates area. That was very uncommon. Both of the elk seemed to be older, two old grandmas. I gave them each names because they seemed to move in the area and we saw them often. I named one Moma Mick and the other Mammy, after my two grandmothers. Again I had no idea that we would become friends or that they would look for me to help them survive. I would talk to both of them, and they did seem happy when they saw me. They'd squeak little noises at me, wag their tails, and one would approach me and let me pet her nose. I felt really small when these huge animals walked toward me, but I never felt threatened. I could see they weren't going to be around too long, especially Moma Mick because she was older. She was thin and frail. My first indication that something was wrong was when we witnessed the two elk eating turkey bones. I didn't think elk were carnivores, but these two were. They had to be lacking something in their diet. For two years they would remain close to our yard or the upper cemetery.

Once, after we lost our beloved game warden Phil Mason, another young warden came by and asked us about the two large "birds" we had in our yard. Robert told him they were old and decided to live in the area and our yard. The warden laughed. We told him they were hard on our plants, but we felt sorry for them and didn't try to make them unwelcomed. The young warden seemed to appreciate that we cared for these two old souls. He got into his truck and left.

The two cow elk were inseparable, constantly together, often seen licking each other's face, and otherwise showing affection to one another. It was easy to see they truly loved each other. Moma Mick and I had bonded. Mammy was more standoffish, but I could scratch Moma Mick's large beautiful head and rub her neck. They won my heart. Finally, one cold winter day I noticed Moma Mick was not getting up. She just laid on the ground with her head up. Mammy stood over her, and I spent several hours each day and night with her, trying to get her to eat until I finally lost her. I cried and cried, she was so sweet and I knew I'd miss her. Mammy stayed for about three days after Moma Mick died. I tried to keep her close, but she disappeared. I worried she had gone off and died. One summer day Robert and I took a hike and we ran into Mammy. She looked good and greeted us as if to say hello. It was great to see her again, but she never returned to our yard.

CHAPTER 5

Meeting Sweety

It was during the summer of 1994 when I had my first meeting with Sweety. I didn't have a clue how this meeting was going to touch my life. I had no way of knowing that one day I would be sitting here trying to write a true story about a chance meeting with a wild animal that would turn into a ten-year friendship. A story about a deer and me, how crazy.

Seeing fawns in our area in the summer isn't real common, usually bears frequent the area and the does keep their young as far away as possible. That summer, however, we were seeing a few fawns; and like everyone, every time we'd see one, the ohhhh's and ahhhh's would come out of our mouths. Not many animals are more precious than a baby deer.

What a busy summer. Both Robert and I were working constantly. If we weren't at our jobs, we were making yard ornaments to sell. I had two jobs – working at the post office and as a janitor for the school. I looked forward to getting home and being with my family. Since I was running in fifty different directions, a quick glance at the fawns was about all I could squeeze in. I wanted to take photographs and did manage to get some; but our camera wasn't much, and it was usually at dusk when the does would move their little one's through our yard. There was one set of twin fawns that seemed to always get my attention, even if I had a million things to do. They were so cute, and one was just unique. What a personality. They were little brothers. One had a dark little face and one had a slightly lighter face. Bounce, bounce, bounce, leap, bolt, and play like crazy. They were entertaining each time we saw them. I felt sorry for the mama; she had her hands full, especially with the lighter faced fawn. He was a little demon. I saw her many times try to get away from him when he wanted to nurse in excess. He'd stiffen his little legs and she would literally drag him. He would hold on to her for dear life. Poor Mama, he'd even box her with his two front legs, he demanded to be fed. He was a little boss, and throughout that little boss's life he would be bossing me.

Robert and I loved watching that little fawn; his personality was so different from the other fawns in the area. He not only was a beautiful little guy, but he had a magnetic personality to go along with all his other assets. His brother, a smaller much shyer little fawn, was also very beautiful. I understood his timidity with a brother like that. Big brother was in charge, and there was no getting around that fact. I always hoped the timid fawn would get a chance to nurse. That unruly brother was selfish and wanted his tummy to be filled first and insisted on it. They had their share of fights; the shy little fawn always the loser, yet he would eventually get to nurse. We also noticed a protective side of the bigger brother, which was good to see. With other animals in the area, and many trying to push each other around, it seemed the tough little guy would put his ears back and chase off anyone who might threaten his little brother. You could almost read his thoughts as he would stomp and jump at another deer or fawn, making it clear they would have to deal with him if they caused any trouble. We had no idea how meeting these two young fawns was going to touch our lives. The way Robert and I both felt about mule deer and hunting would change drastically, all because of a very special brown-eyed, four-legged, little creature and his shy little brother.

CHAPTER 6

Orphans

Most evenings I would get home by 6:00 or 6:30. I'd work at the Post Office during the days, clean the school after I got off of work, then try and fix dinner and be mom and wife. I wasn't really prepared for what was about to happen. It was October and the aspen leaves had begun to change and were beautiful bright colors of yellow, red, and orange. I loved fall. Colorado is gorgeous this time of year. We had two early snowfalls already. Most had melted, yet underneath some of the trees lay some of the white soft snow that was hidden from the sun. The two little fawns and their mom still bounced through our yard, playfully catching our attention whenever they graced us with their appearance. It was also the beginning of hunting season, so we not only had this family of deer, but we also had many more coming down out of the mountains to safety. Bruiser had showed up, as well as King, Little King, and many

y & Sweety with a friend.

others. I guarantee the smart bucks were down and out of the hills. It was always so exciting to see them and good to know they had survived another year. I'd be waiting on each one to show up, hoping and praying they had made it.

Whenever I got a chance (which was usually only on Sundays) to take a hike, Robert and I would head up into the hills. We never liked to walk the "people trails;" but we wanted to get completely away from everything, so that was our best bet. We ran into the mom and fawns several times. I would talk to them, and the fawns would perk their little ears up and seem to listen to every word I'd say. Their mom seemed to trust us and would never run if we got close, yet we never purposely tried to approach them. We knew her job was to protect her babies, and we never wanted her to feel threatened by us. The fawns, especially the brave one, wanted to get close to us. They were so curious and would often be following us as we passed by them. Then their mom would call them. However, getting the brave one's attention was sometimes nearly impossible, so I would turn and tell the little sweet baby he'd better go back. I swear this little guy understood English. He would trot right back to his mom, but would watch us as we disappeared.

November hit with a vengeance. We had snow, wind, and even a sickness in our family. Beth, my boss, my sister in-law, and old friend had been diagnosed with breast cancer. It was bad. Nine lymph nodes showed cancer, her survival rate wasn't good, and her treatment plan was going to be severe; it alone could kill her. She was so afraid, and we were afraid for her. In an instant life changed. Beth needed me full time at the office while she received treatment. I gave my notice to the school, knowing I could no longer do both jobs. Beth needed me to run the office and I had never run it without her. I was afraid, but wanted to do the best I could do so she didn't have to worry.

What else could happen? Well something did and I was not ready for it. My two little fawns showed up in our yard alone. What had happened to their mom? What was I going to do now? Robert and I searched for the doe. Where in the world was she? I loved those little guys. I did not want them to have lost their mother; but, after a couple of days of not seeing her, I knew they were orphaned. I was certain that in my yard they felt safe. I was a friend to them. Seeing Robert and I all summer, they knew we were not out to harm them. I hoped another doe might try and adopt them; but, as the days passed, I watched as all of the does ran them off. I found myself going out and chasing other deer away. I began making little meals for them and making sure they ate. I was their only friend. I wasn't sure how I would take care of them. My plate was full and my responsibilities were huge. Now I had two small babies that needed my help also. They had won my heart. I would try and be mom to them.

Robert and I both knew the fawns were still nursing, but they weren't totally dependent on their mother. They were both eating grass and leaves, and if we threw an apple or carrot they would come and gobble it up quickly. Still, whether they would survive without their mother was a huge concern to us both. We were gone more than we were home. Should we call the Division of Wildlife and see what they would do? Robert had just heard a story on the local news about a couple who had found a fawn and the division took it in because it was still spotted. A fawn still having spots seemed to be the key at that time as to whether it could survive on its own. Our two fawns had lost their spots, and they would probably be looked at as too old to take in. We both agreed then that it would be up to us to see that they did get food. We could only hope that a predator didn't get them, but we could keep them from starving. We were thankful that they had already learned to trust us. We would do what we could. We agreed that at least we would try, and hopefully they would survive.

I began by mixing bird seed, sunflower seed, and a small amount of 4-way grain with a little corn. Variety, I felt, was best. I'd try and give them all the vital nutrients I believed they needed. I also cut up carrots and some apples. I wanted them to get good nutrition, and yet I didn't want them to solely depend on me. I am a strong believer that when food is plentiful God knows what is best for his creatures, and I believe they should eat his food. God gave us brains for a reason, but he can only do so much. He has his hands full taking care of us all. Robert and I never helped the deer when we saw God doing his work. The winters here can be absolutely brutal on wildlife, especially when the snow and ice builds up and prevents the deer from being able to dig for their natural food. The adult deer have a tough enough time. Left on their own, these two fawns would find it impossible.

I began to try to throw food to the small fawns and separate them from the larger

Sweety and me.

deer. This was not an easy task, and sometimes it was dangerous. Bruiser thought he should be taken care of, and his attitude with the fawns wasn't the best. I loved old Bruiser, but I chased him off with a broom. The fawns needed my help more than he did.

It wasn't long before the little, brave, adorable fawn was eating out of my hands and licking my face. He would wag his little tail and several times he'd lie down next to me and let me scratch his neck. He was so sweet. Because of his loving nature, I named him "Sweety." The other fawn had a totally opposite disposition. I couldn't get close to him. I could throw food and he would eat it, but he would not let me touch him. He wanted to come close, but something stopped him. He would hide behind a bush or tree, sneak as quietly as he could to grab a bite, and then jump back into hiding. He was smart though and quick. He was a little sneaky when he approached me or the other deer. He would get the food that he wanted one way or the other. That earned him the name of "Sly." He was a pretty smart little guy. As busy and crazy as life was, now we had more to do and more to worry about. Sweety and Sly – Robert and I had adopted two more babies.

I'm a worrier. Robert always says if I didn't have something to worry about I would go out and find something. I have to agree with him…I laugh about that sometimes, and I also cry about it sometimes. Worry is a huge waste of my time and energy. I feel guilty always praying to God to take care of everything; I'm sure my problems are small compared to all He has to deal with.

It was when our daughter Jennifer was born that I really began the worry, worrying constantly. I guarantee there were no more nights when I would sleep an entire night. No, I must have awakened twenty times a night just to lean close to her and make sure she was okay. Life took a radical turn from that moment on. I was responsible for another life. Growing up in the situation that I did, sometimes, many times, us kids didn't know where our mom and dad were. I wanted to be the best mom I could be – be there for her and pray she would always be proud of me. That's another story though.

All of a sudden here Robert and I were, adopting two babies; maybe they weren't human, but boy were they ever special. Huge brown beautiful eyes; those eyes would win anyone's heart. And when they looked at me for help, that's exactly what they received. Sleepless nights hit with a vengeance; the wind would blow, the snow would fall, and the coyote's would scream, and I was up and running out the door, praying the coyotes weren't killing my babies. When the temperatures were bitter, I was miserable, wishing I could put the two fawns in a shed. Sweety would have gone into a shed or would have even come into our house, but not Sly. I had no choice but to put their fate into God's hands. What a cold, cold winter it was, one that chilled you to the bone. I could feel my breath freeze. We had many nights that fell to thirty below zero. Sweety's and Sly's little faces would be frosty every morning, their eye lashes and noses would have small icicles hanging from them. I'd grab a towel and rub Sweety down, wishing I could get a hold of Sly, but that was out of the question. Those two babies were tough and I thanked the dear Lord that they were. I also was so thankful that they both seemed so smart. Nature is just amazing. Morning and night I would go out and call their names and in a second or two I would see two little fawns bouncing my way. I would have their food prepared in a bowl and they would fill their little bellies. While they ate I stood guard, ready to run off the other deer that might try to take their food. This was a daily ritual that worked. Thank God, we would make it through our first winter together. The sweet little orphans would survive without their mother.

Chapter 7

Spring and Summer

Spring was finally here, and we were so ready. Sunshine was a welcome sight. Winter just drug on and on; it seemed to last forever. Snow-covered fields became bare, and the brown grasses began to show new life as sprouts of green weaved their way toward the blue sky. Warm winds blew and felt so good on our skin. The robins returned to our yard. They sang the most beautiful song, and along with all the other birds, we had a symphony. The marmots began poking their heads out of their winter dens; their chirping also was welcomed. Like all my four-legged creatures, they too ran to me as if to say hello, we are back, where are the carrots? After six months of hibernation I had a small army of hungry animals. Marmots are such gentle animals. In all the years we have spent with them, they have never attempted to bite us or act aggressive in any way. They climb into our laps like cats and let us scratch their ears and pet them. The only time they might nip you is if they mistakenly take your finger to be a carrot. Of course I had my favorite marmots – Mom, Moose, Big Guy, and Broken Finger. Broken Finger earned her name because when she would reach for food her little hand looked as if she were flipping you off. We had Mom for nearly twelve years. She was the boss of the marmots and pretty much ruled who would be allowed in our yard. She and Moose both kept the population under control. It was amazing to see how they worked together. Sometimes it seemed cruel, but I believe they knew way more than I did, so I never interfered when Moose or Mom would take another marmot out.

Moose and Mom ruled our yard.

Sweety and Sly weren't real excited about our new guests, and the feelings were mutual. What were these little brown creatures and why were they eating their carrots? Who did they think they were and why was the fawn's new mom feeding them the carrots she usually fed her two little deer? You could see Sweety's dislike toward them. Even though he had no antler growth, he threatened them as if he had swords, and he used his small hooves as fists several times. I wondered if the fawns would stay all summer. They were like puppies. Had I ruined them from knowing they were wild animals? This really worried me because I had heard many people say I would take their wild nature out of them. I half wanted them to stay so I could keep my eye on the both of them, yet my heart knew that wasn't right. I didn't want to be responsible for them not being able to make it in the wilderness.

The new aspen leaves appearing all over the mountains were always great to see – not only for me but for the deer that had come down from higher up last fall. They must have loved to eat the lime green leaves, because the instant they popped out, the deer were gone. Well guess who else was gone? Sweety and Sly took off with the herd. Would I ever see the two again? I was heartbroken, but yet I was happy. I was glad they felt they were big enough to go out on their own. Now I would have to wait until the new green leaves turned golden in the fall with the hope of seeing my two babies again.

Summer was crazy. Beth was still taking treatments, and I was mostly alone at work. The post office gets insanely busy in the summer months. In the winters we only have about 500 residents, but in the summer the town grows to about 2,000. Fourth of July is a huge tourist draw, the fishing is great, and just the beauty of Lake City offers so much to attract tourists. Our daughter was a teenager and was in her first serious relationship, so all in all both Robert and I had our hands full. Time to just hang around the yard was rare. To get a day off from work in the summer was not easy. This summer there would be no days off. With Beth not in the office, and my being there alone, it wasn't going to happen. Spending time with my family was what I needed to take advantage of if given the chance. Spending time with the animals had to be my least concern.

Beth had gone through so much – a stem cell transplant, chemotherapy and radiation; but the treatments were working, and that was the most important thing. I missed her being with me at work. I had many days I didn't believe I could do it alone. I found myself in tears on several occasions. Beth would show up to help when she could. She had been through hell. Her skin coloring was bad. She had a gray look to her face, and her hair was gone; but she was tough. She was going to make it, and I knew soon she'd be back taking charge of the office.

I thought of Sweety and Sly often and wondered if they both were alright. We had seen several little new babies running around the area. It sure made me miss my two little ones. Bears were making regular visits to our yard. The town transfer station is just down the hill from us, not far at all. Bears were always hanging out there. Several sets of cubs were running around, and the tourists loved getting to see them. I let several groups of people go to my yard to see the marmots, and some would also get to see a bear passing through. This seemed to make their vacations. They would be thrilled; they couldn't thank us enough. It excited them so much to see these animals. They would tell us they had never had a chance in the city to see such beautiful creatures, unless they went to a zoo. We are blessed in so many ways, so lucky to get to see these wild animals. Even our birds kept the tourists entertained for hours. Some women asked us if they could just sit in our yard for awhile, as it was therapy for them. A "healing yard" they called it; how nice to hear. Several asked us if we wanted to sell our place; but no, that wasn't going to happen. We would laugh about it, but you could see some of these folks really wanted to buy our home and especially buy our yard. They were dead serious.

I told many of the visitors about the experience I'd had last winter with the two fawns, and how I was praying I'd see them again. I even had a few in tears (including me) when I talked about them. I showed pictures of all the deer to a number of people, and they sure seemed impressed with some of the pictures of our bucks. Some asked if they could hunt in my backyard. Ha! Well you know my answer to that – No, and No, and No again and again. Just the thought of hunting season sent chills down my spine. Sweety and Sly were small yet, but they would grow up; they could be hunted. What an awful thought. I didn't know then just how much I was going to dread hunting seasons in the years ahead. Their well-being would become a horrible nightmare for me. This year, though, the fawns would be much too young to attract hunters. Please let them come home. I prayed for God to give me another chance to be with them and let them survive another winter.

Our yard is sort of a tourist attraction for viewing animals and wildflowers.

Chapter 8

Sweety and Sly Come Home

The aspens were beautiful that fall, but to me they are always beautiful. There were a lot more red leaves seen against the golden leaves shimmering in the wind. Tourists come from all over the United States just to see Colorado's magnificent fall colors. Most Sundays Robert and I would pack a snack and water and hike up into the mountains. The bow hunters and muzzleloaders had already finished their fall hunt. Next would be rifle season. We took advantage of this time. It was quiet and undisturbed, peaceful. We would come upon bobcats, bears, deer, and some elk; but it was always hard to get close to the elk. Robert had bought a better camera, so we hoped to get better pictures. We would always carry our binoculars and spend the days just looking around. This was therapy for the both of us. We would deeply breathe in the fresh air and take in the beauty that surrounded us with a smile on our faces. We were away from the office, away from work, escaping into wonderland.

Bruiser was the first buck to show up when the guns started firing in the hills. I was always thrilled to see him and welcomed him back into our yard. A red apple was usually the welcoming gift, and it was always appreciated. As tough as he was, and as tough as he acted, he was gentle around me. I asked him where all his buddies were, and if he'd seen Sweety and Sly. I so wished he could talk back to me; even though if that deer could have talked, I'm sure not one nice thing would come out of his mouth about the other bucks. He had a personality like Groucho Marx and was not the most friendly fella. I loved him though, and he was special.

The last day of the second hunting season, oh thank the Lord, Robert and I woke to deer tracks on our porch. I jumped out of bed and ran to the window. A small forked antlered buck was staring through the window of our door. It was Sweety, no doubt about it. I opened the door and threw my arms around his small neck. He was home. I looked for Sly and at first didn't see him. I wished the world could have watched Sweety and I seeing each other again, as it was wonderful.

I hugged his little neck, kissed his cute nose, and he licked my face and arms. I grabbed him some treats, then looked around to see if I could see Sly. I noticed three small bucks heading down off of our neighbor Burton Smith's hill. They were all the same size, they also were yearlings. I knew Sly was one of them. I recognized his dark little face, though another little buck had a dark face also. Sly's face was wider and stronger looking. Sly didn't come running to me, but he sure knew who I was, and I saw his little tail wag as he stood there patiently waiting for a treat. I ended up giving treats to all four small bucks. This would become a regular sight. We named each small buck – Sweety, Sly, Beauty, and Whitey. They soon earned another name, "The gang of four." They were together constantly. Little buddies, the friendship between these young deer would continue throughout their lives.

To witness this was an amazing learning experience for Robert and me. Just like humans, these animals had chosen their friends. They would wash each other's faces with their huge long tongues and play deer games, which consisted of running, jumping, and playing chase. They would gather in a corner of our yard and lie down to rest. We were fascinated by them. Each little buck had something special about him. Sweety was absolutely great. He had personality like no other. I could see – even as young as he was – what a beautiful animal he was growing up to be. Sweety's eyes had such an honest and trusting look to them. Many times you can tell by looking in a dog's eyes if it can to be trusted or not. I could look into Sweety's eyes and feel his love toward me. He was my puppy. Sweety followed me like a dog would. In many ways though, Sweety was more gentle. He did not bite or bark. He seemed to find comfort in my being close to him. While he was bonding with the other bucks, he and I were building a friendship like I had never had. Sly was Sly, still a little nervous and shy. Sly's eyes were honest too. I felt he could look right through me. I could see he badly wanted to trust me, but something inside of Sly had made him fearful. I had to be very gentle with him, even when tossing his food toward him.

We named the other dark-faced buck "Beauty." Beauty was a dancer. He would prance and jump and shake his head up and down. Watching him dance for a treat was so enjoyable. The way Beauty would hold his little head up high and shake it around was beautiful. We watched and laughed as he put on a show for us. He would have won Dancing With The Stars. What a talent Beauty had. The fourth buck, we named "Whitey." Whitey was just their little buddy with a very white face. He would cuddle close to each of the others; kind of a follower. It seemed that Sweety was the boss or the leader of the Pack. Whatever Sweety did, or wherever Sweety went, his buddies were right behind him.

Chapter 9

The Gang of Four

Sweety was born a leader. I'm not sure if it was because he was orphaned so young in life or if it was just his nature. He was only a year old and already had a following. He demanded respect even as little as he was; and he got it from the whole herd. When we watched the gang of four play their deer games, sparring, running, boxing and whatever, Sweety was always the victor. Watching them taught us how a deer would get his status in the herd. Sweety was aggressive enough and strong enough to lay claim as king of his gang. His broad shoulders rippled with muscles already. He could push much larger bucks than him clear across our entire yard.

Beth had come back to work, but it would be some time before she gained all her strength back. She would still need me to help her out at the office for quite

Gang of Four.

awhile. Getting to spend a lot of time with Sweety and Sly was hard for me to do. I didn't know it then, but it would be awhile before life would return to normal. The treatments Beth had to endure would take a toll on her body, and we were looking at several years before she would feel normal again. The next several winters would pretty much repeat the one before. Sweety and his gang would show up in the fall, as well as Bruiser, King, and the others. I would go through the worry of hunting season, and the worry of predators. Sweety and I grew closer each winter, so close that by the time he was the age of four, if I were in my yard or taking a walk, he was right beside me. Throughout his early years we bonded like two dear friends. He depended on me, and I depended on him. He brought me laughter when I was sad. Like cats often know when their owner is depressed, Sweety seemed to also know when I was. Instead of having a dog, I had a deer. Sweety was my pet; and from September until Spring showed its face, Sweety was with me whenever the chance was given us.

The winter of 96-97 was a harsh winter. Snow began falling and wouldn't quit. This year Phil Mason saw the need for the D.O.W. to help feed the deer. It was also the year that my daughter was getting married. What a wonderful guy she'd found. We were so lucky to have him in our family. This was also a winter when I was to be stalked for months by some crazed man. I was trying to feed the deer, prepare for a wedding, and scared out of my mind by this man.

The man had gotten angry at me at work over not putting a postal stamp on something for him. I wasn't allowed to do what he wanted, but that didn't seem to matter. He began writing threatening letters and, several times, was seen near our home by our neighbors. They once thought it strange to find him in a short-sleeved tee shirt, smoking a cigarette while it was freezing outside, standing just a short way from my yard. They witnessed him standing and walking around the edge of our yard many times. I had no idea he was even there. Several of the letters he wrote described the inside of my house and even talks between my daughter and I. Knowing he had been so close without our knowledge was terrifying. The police couldn't do anything unless he attacked me or entered our home. He was known for stalking women. Even at my place of work, he would park his van and just sit there. Once he came in and kicked all the boxes around in our office. I crawled on the floor to avoid him seeing me and called the sheriff. Bill Denison was a deputy then and came instantly, throwing the stalker up against the wall and threatening him if he didn't leave me alone. That was all that could be done. Later we did find items of mine missing from our house, personal items. This gave the cops more evidence, and they were able to ban him from Lake City. The most comfort I had during this time was that I knew Bruiser and Sweety were in my yard. I believed without a doubt if that man would have tried to hurt me as I left my locked house and walked through or around my yard, they would have protected me. I wished they could have barked like a dog. Their antlers, though, were threatening; and I'd seen both Bruiser and Sweety run off many an animal. When they were angry, the world knew it. That was a comfort to me.

Jennifer and Justin were married and it all went off without a hitch. We were blessed to have a great son in-law. His family had been friends of ours for years.

That year the deer survived the harsh winter with the help of so many of the town's people. Phil thanked us all and gave hats and posters to all who had helped. Sweety and Sly looked great and hadn't lost too many pounds. I loved each and every minute Sweety and I were able to spend together. Knowing they needed us seemed to make it even better. The deer appreciated us. Their eyes told you they were thankful. The D.O.W. appreciated our efforts. It was a group effort and very rewarding.

Robert Hurd & Larry Cadwell opening Engineer Pass.

Chapter 10

Bruiser

Summer went well, and another winter was behind us. The gang of four had left with the rest of the herd in April, and once again the golden leaves were falling from the aspens. Our daughter and son in-law had bought property and built their house about a half mile from us. Life seemed almost perfect. Beth was back at work more, my stalker was gone, and my daughter was happily married. Sweety and Sly had survived the winter, which was so very important to me. I'd survived another busy summer and was ready for everything to slow down. I was ready and waiting for the deer to return.

During the previous winter I had gotten to know several new deer. It seemed the original gang of four grew larger all the time. There was Squirt, who had the funniest little crooked set of antlers. Squirt had huge eyes and giant long

ears. He was one funny looking little buck. There was Trouble, a young buck who just seemed to annoy all the others. There were also Buster, Too Cute, Magraw, Little King, Slick, and Odd Ball. Odd Ball was just strange looking. He was born with one antler that always took the shape of a unicorn, while his other was normal. Giving them names helped me identify them, but also made me care more for them. I hoped they would all show up in the fall. I started

Bruiser was the first mule deer I ever became friends with. He didn't like other deer.

bugging the poor hunters. I was almost begging them not to kill my Sweety. I would show pictures of him at work from the year before and pray that they would recognize him and not shoot him. I put a lot of pressure on them. Some hunters asked me to tie a ribbon around his neck or ask the D.O.W to see if they could protect him. Our local wildlife officer, Phil Mason, told me that he was afraid tying a ribbon around Sweety might draw more attention to him. He said a pet elk in Boulder, Colorado had been killed like that. I agreed. Some idiot just out of spite might kill him. I would just give my worries to God and pray that Sweety would survive another hunting season.

As usual, the first buck down from the high country was my Bruiser. Oh, but how he had changed. What a sad, sad old man he was. His once long, sword-like antlers had declined dramatically. The once proud buck now stood with his head hanging low. He no longer ruled my yard. He backed away from the larger, younger bucks and avoided any confrontation. Instead of him being my protector, I became his. I wrapped my arms around him and could feel his bones. He had lost a huge amount of weight. We were pretty close friends, so he let me check his teeth. I tugged at his jaw until he opened his mouth. I stuck my fingers in and felt all around inside his mouth. His teeth were worn down so badly that he had nothing left with which to chew his food. Robert and I both knew that this was common in older deer. We also realized it could be fatal. Bruiser was so undernourished already. He was slowly starving to death.

The gang of four showed up with new friends. Sweety came directly to me. Oh my goodness, Sweety was beautiful. A four by four, and if you counted his eye guards, he was a five. His horns were thick. Sweety was a trophy. We welcomed each other as we'd done every year. He was so much larger, and wrapping my arms around his neck was a little scary. I was so glad to see him though, I had to hug him. I wondered if he'd let me. He could kill me so easy with one swipe of those antlers. He licked my face, what sloppy kisses, and I threw my arms around him. I probably could have jumped on his back. No matter what I did to him, Sweety seemed alright with it all. I knew in my heart I needed to respect him. He was much stronger than I was.

Sweety was now the ruler of my yard – the king of his gang. Bruiser stood back and watched the magnificent Sweety take over his kingdom. I was sad for Bruiser but happy for Sweety. Sweety showed Bruiser respect, and I was very grateful for that. The other bucks also showed Bruiser respect. Sweety seemed to understand when I gave Bruiser attention and not him. I could see he didn't really like it, but he accepted it. This made me love Sweety even more. I saw so many gentle sides to Sweety. What an amazing animal he was. To think that the entire herd realized that Bruiser was near the end of his life! There was no doubt in my mind that each one knew of his situation. They truly respected each other.

Trying to get Bruiser to eat was a difficult job. I would grind carrots and apples and mix them with bird seed. Then I would separate him from the other deer and hand feed him. I would have to keep my hand beneath his lower jaw, as food would fall out of his mouth. In two weeks I saw a huge difference in Bruiser's condition. He was definitely stronger. The rutting season was in full swing, and all the bucks were chasing the does. Bruiser began showing interest in the girls, and he disappeared for some time. I was worried because I didn't believe he was strong enough to do this, but it was his nature and what he wanted to do. Sweety was a "romancer." He had the does, and he was not having to chase them. During the rut he might leave for a day or two, but never for very long. He would leave just long enough to gather up more does and head back where he knew he'd be taken care of. Sure enough, I saw a lot of does I'd never seen before. Sweety gave his women a huge amount of attention, licking their necks and making sure they had the first bite to eat. He was a very considerate man, a gentleman. The does didn't run from him; they backed up to him. Needless to say, I know there are a lot of little Sweetys running around today. What a bloodline. I hoped he would be the daddy to every fawn. I could never have too many Sweetys.

It was Christmas Eve when a very thin, close to death, old and tired buck came back to my yard. I was in a state of panic. I didn't want to lose my old friend Bruiser. The next six weeks I spent many evenings sitting next to him and trying to get him to eat. Sweety would lie about ten feet away from Bruiser and me and, once in awhile, put his ears back and snort. Sweety was slightly jealous of the attention Bruiser was getting. Sly still stayed close to Sweety, and as yet I couldn't pet him, so he wasn't as jealous. None of the other deer seemed jealous either. Without a doubt, Sweety was taking it the hardest.

Robert didn't know what to do with me, but he kept saying, "Karen, Bruiser has lived a good life. You've done all you can do." I spent so much time with

Bruiser when I got home from work that I didn't have much time for Robert. I was thankful that Jennifer didn't need my attention like she used to. I was so consumed with trying to save Bruiser. Robert had to shoot several coyotes that began hanging out near our yard. The coyotes knew Bruiser was weak and saw an easy meal. Sleeping was nearly impossible. I would jump up and look out my window as many times as I could drag myself out of bed. Bruiser was always lying beneath the big pine tree in our yard. On one cold February morning I woke to find Bruiser gone. We searched that morning, but could not find him. After work we searched again. Not far from my yard, about 200 yards away to the south side off of the road and down the embankment, we found Bruiser's eaten body. In one night Bruiser had been eaten. All that was left was his head and his small shrunken antlers. His bones were bare of flesh. I was an absolute mess. He was a special old guy, and I loved him, and I would miss him like crazy. I cried so hard I was sick. The dirt was frozen hard, but Robert and I dug until we had a grave and buried Bruiser's remains in our backyard.

Young Brusier.

Bruiser in his last year of life. His antlers had declined dramatically.

Chapter 11

Playing Games

It took a while to quit crying over Bruiser. I cried over him like I'd lost one of my dogs. I had lost so many family members. I should have been tougher, but it seems as I aged I was weaker. Death scared me so much, and going through the loss terrified me. People die, animals die. I knew that truth more than I wanted to. Death was the one thing I knew you couldn't change. Every effort in the world would not change death. I couldn't breathe life back into anyone that I loved and lost, no matter how bad I wanted to. Where I got comfort was from knowing there were years when I had made Bruiser's life a little bit easier. That old man loved me and I loved him.

Sweety was the only one not really bothered by Bruiser's death. Nope, he now had my full attention. He must have known that I was sad; and in his way he tried to comfort me by laying his huge body down next to where I sat on my front porch and leaning his monstrous head on my knees. I scratched his ears, but had to be real careful because his antlers were big enough to poke my eyes out. He was a lot larger than a cat or dog. I cried even harder as I talked to him. "Sweety you can't die, ever. I can't lose you," I said. Bruiser's dying almost killed me. Sweety if something happens to you, I don't know if I can handle it. What had I gotten myself into? I felt that anyone going through what I was experiencing with these wild animals would love them like I did. I got up and moved Sweety's big head from my knees, went and got him a treat, kissed his nose a couple of times, then turned around to find Sly closer to me than usual. What a surprise. "Well what are you doing little buddy?" I asked. I had a slice of apple and reached out to Sly. He stretched his neck out as far as he could and with a quick nibble he took the apple from my hand. All this time and now he decided to trust me; or was he too trying to comfort me? It was great. I'd worked hard to gain his trust and thought it was a losing battle. Now Sly made the move without me pursuing it. I ran in the house and cut up a couple more apples. Now both Sweety and Sly were eating out of my hands, and I was smiling. They made me forget for awhile the hurt I'd been going through.

It didn't take long to completely turn Sly into a very loving animal. Once I'd won his trust, he would walk and run beside me in my yard. Sweety would walk with me, but he wouldn't run. No, he was not going to waste his energy chasing me around the yard. I'm not sure what was happening, but it wasn't long before several bucks would run up and down the hill in the back of our yard with me. I had a ball. There were two young bucks I called Crooked Horn and Buster. One would be on my left and one would be on my right, both running right beside me. This became a game, and Sly had started it all. The only problem was I now could no longer walk on our dirt road. Those crazy deer followed me; they wanted to play chase. So I began walking and running on their deer trails with them. I'd get to laughing because it was so much fun to have these guys playing with me in this amazing way. I could stretch out my arms and touch the deer. Up the mountain and down the mountain, we ran together. I felt as if I were playing with friends as I'd done in school. Robert watched us several times. He worried I'd get hurt, but he knew I was having so much fun. He laughed as he watched us. He and Sweety both patiently waited for me to tire and come take care of them.

I mentioned the deer games one day when I was visiting with Don Cardin. He warned me I was going to get hurt or killed if I wasn't careful. I told him how crazy it was to have these good-sized bucks running right next to me, kicking, jumping, and literally playing. I told him that I had seen how aggressive they were at times with each other, but they never acted aggressive toward me. I admitted I might get surprised one day and get knocked to China by one of them. I think at times Don thought this woman is out of her mind, completely nuts. I told Don, you know if I do ever get hurt, I think I'd rather be hurt by one of them than in a car wreck or being hurt by another human. I still believe I'd rather have a wild animal kill me than die in a lot of other ways. I believe they would get the job done and my suffering wouldn't be an issue. I told Don about Sweety not running with me. Don said, Sweety was too smart to act like that, and I knew Sweety was too proud and thought we were idiots up there chasing each other. Sweety would watch us and even shake his big head, like what in the world is she doing? I'd call for him, but he'd just wait until I was exhausted from running and went and sat down next to him. I felt Don liked hearing the deer stories. Don was stern with me. He didn't beat around the bush on anything. A very honest, straight-forward man. I could trust Don and I valued his friendship. His disapproval of my running with the deer was understood. He was right and I was crazy. I was just having a lot of fun and felt like a kid playing with these animals.

Several does had also befriended me by now. I had Girlfriend, Granny, Little Brownie, and one small fawn we named Feisty. I wish you could have seen how each one of those deer had a different personality. FEISTY, this name fit her perfect. She would stomp her feet and throw her head around and dance. She had more energy than every one of them. We loved watching her. She would take off running and get the whole herd upset. She would run nonstop for thirty minutes straight. Some of the deer would decide to chase her, and as little as she was, she out ran each one. I guess she was our race horse.

Girlfriend

Feisty

One day Robert and I had to go and get groceries in Gunnison and on our way home, as we turned up the cemetery road, we saw Sweety and about twenty other deer on the hillside. I unrolled my window and yelled " Hey, Sweety! You are too close to the highway. Get away from the road!" Sweety's ears perked up and, as we tried to drive off, Sweety began running beside our car. I looked back and the whole herd was chasing our car. Robert tried to get off to one of the back roads and, as we drove up Cedar Drive Hill, Robert let me out on the top of the hill, so he could get back out on the main road. I could cut across the hillside and have the deer go with me. It worked. Sweety and his loyal followers walked and ran down the hill with me, and we met Robert in our yard. I'd have given anything to have that on film.

Beauty in velvet.

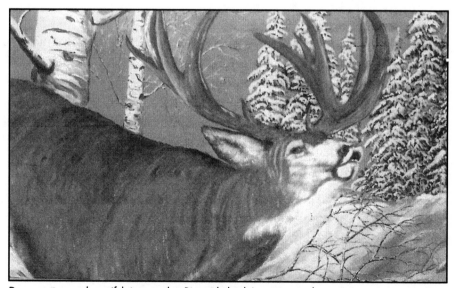

Dempsey was so beautiful, just another Riverside buck I was inspired to paint.

Chapter 12

Going to be Grandparents

On my daughter's first wedding anniversary, March 12, 1998, Jennifer and Justin called us and asked Robert and I if we could come over because they had some news they wanted to share with us. It was fantastic news. We were going to be grandparents. Jen was expecting. They both were nervous, but Robert and I were so excited. The baby was expected to arrive by the end of October or early November. It was nearly spring and I was glad the weather was getting nicer, since we had to go so far to visit Jen's doctor. Even in the months the baby was due, the weather could be bad.

We had lots of plans, new plans. I was glad everything was timed like it was. Sweety, Sly, the gang, and a few others were still hanging around, but it wouldn't be long before they would be gone for the summer. We had had a good winter except for the loss of Bruiser. The bucks had started losing their antlers, and they looked pretty funny. It completely changed their personalities. The tough acting animals seemed much less threatening to the other deer. No more pushing around was allowed. The does battled back. It seemed the small bucks were the last to lose their antlers, so they really acted tough toward the older guys. It was fun to watch and see how the loss of their weapons turned their lives upside down. I enjoyed this time of year because they all seemed more mild mannered. It was pleasant. I love spring more than any time of the year. Work was slow, and I could get some time off. Robert and I love to hike, so we would spend as much time as possible in the hills. We love to antler hunt, and especially to hunt for the antlers of the bucks we knew. I had about five years of Bruisers antlers, from the biggest to the last set – the small declining antlers that took his pride away. I had Sweety's first small forked antlers, and his second, and third sets; but this year I only had found one of Sweety's antlers, and I had to walk miles looking for it. I was heartbroken, as I treasured them. I had heard rumors that one of my neighbors found one on their front porch that fit the description of what Sweety's antler looked like, so I had given up looking.

By the middle of April the deer were gone, and we were busy planning for our grandbaby. The marmots had come out of their holes and were invading our yard. Robert and I worked hard to get the yard in shape and only planted plants that the marmots would not eat. They cleared every dandelion out of our yard. They were great for clearing weeds for us. Robert planted peonies, and he is pretty well known in town for his beautiful peonies. Neither the deer nor the marmots liked the taste of peonies, so we had every color and they were magnificent. We had lilacs, crab apple trees, and cherry trees. The deer in the winter were hard on many of our trees, so we would go to great lengths to protect them. The bears were just as bad in the summer, for some reason, I guess just being mean. They would totally destroy trees by ripping branches off, sometimes completely destroying the entire tree. So we were kept busy keeping the animals out of our yard in the summer. Our yard was our paradise, and we loved it and shared it with many of our friends. Some days we had lines of cars stopping and taking pictures and getting out to meet the marmots. In the summers, our yard was a popular tourist attraction.

Tourists enjoying the marmots.

Chapter 13

Lane and a New Baby

Jennifer was having high blood pressure problems as she entered her seventh month of pregnancy. Her doctor needed to see her more, so he could keep a closer eye on her health. Justin would take her when he could, but he was working at a job where getting time off was nearly impossible. The hours he was putting in were insane. Robert and I wanted to help in any way we could, so we took turns driving her to Gunnison so she could keep her doctor's appointments. Her blood pressure issues were serious, and her doctor began talking of an early inducement. Justin and I both planned to be with her when she delivered. Boy, was I nervous and worried.

Squirt

The deer were late in coming down that fall, so I went through all my usual fears of hunting season. Our local grocery store did most of the processing of meat and often on my way to work I would see a dead elk or dead deer hanging in their shed with the door wide open or the animal laid out on the front porch of the shed. I can't count how many times I feared I'd see Sweety or one of the bucks I knew hanging or lying there. I was scared to death that I would drive off the road or get in an accident if I saw someone I recognized – lifeless. I also was afraid of what I would do. Jump out of the car and tell the hunter what a horrible man or woman they were . . . PROBABLY. It was pretty certain it would be a very ugly scene. God help them, I might get physical. I was under additional stress with my daughter sick; and since I was always under stress at hunting season, I was a complete basket case. This was not a good time of year for me, and my poor husband had pretty much quit hunting. He defiantly gave up deer hunting and took up photographing the deer. Life was much easier for him after he made these changes.

Where was Sweety, Sly, Beauty? Where was the herd? For some reason it took a good snow storm that year to bring them all down. I was a worried mess. There were times I loved Sweety and times I hated him. He was going to give me ulcers or make me grow old before my time. A bull elk or mule deer buck, especially a beautiful trophy buck like Sweety, would always be desirable to a hunter. Also, he would be hunted by predators, and lord only knew if he'd jump in front of a car or get hurt in the wilderness, hung up on a fence, or something. I've seen so many dead deer lying just off the highway. They have it rough. Life for them is not easy.

So I worried, but Sweety finally came back okay and bigger. His antlers were taller and thicker, just absolutely awesome. All the guys were okay. King, oh he was something else. Robert and I both didn't know why, but when he showed up we both teared up. At first we only saw a deer's behind and this huge spread of antlers, so very, very wide. We didn't have to look at his face to know who it was. Maybe we knew he was getting older and knew we'd probably lose him soon. He was breathtakingly beautiful. Squirt was good looking this year too; he had gone from such a funny looking fawn to a very handsome man. Squirt was soon to become Robert's favorite. He thought Squirt's bloodline was the best. He and Don both told me Sweety's front two tines were weak, and that wasn't great in a bloodline. I never listened to them! I was the wrong person to tell that Sweety wasn't perfect.

King had lived over by my daughter's house and was the ruler there. Sweety wasn't too crazy about him and they would avoid each other. When King came in our area, Sweety would do all he could to run him out. I'm not sure if they ever fought each other. King was tough. I'm afraid King may have been wiser than Sweety. He was older and had fought many battles. I know it would have been a tough match.

Sweety was getting very well known in our neighborhood. One gentleman thought he was great and had named him "Elvis." That name was fitting for such a terrific deer. Harold Pate was the gentleman, and we would trade Sweety and Elvis stories back and forth. I was glad Sweety had made more friends, as

I felt they might try and protect him also. I was always searching for protection for him.

The due date for the arrival of our grandbaby was getting nearer, and hunting season was in full swing. Boy, were there a lot of hunters driving through our neighborhood and stopping and staring at my Sweety. I would go out in my yard and say "Please don't hunt him," and I would show them he was a pet. I even jumped in my truck several times and followed the hunters, especially when they took a road I knew was private property. Friends owned it, and the deer liked to be in this little valley a lot. I ran several hunters off of the property. I just was half crazy at this time of year.

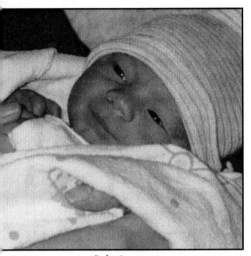

Baby Lane

Jen's blood pressure was not getting any better, so her doctor suggested early delivery. We left for Gunnison on the 25th of October to have her labor induced. The inducement didn't work as the doctor had hoped. I watched my daughter in complete agony for three days. She crawled on the floor of the room we had rented and was in so much pain. I prayed and prayed for her to hurry and have this baby. Finally, the doctor tried once again to induce her, and it was successful. An easy labor it wasn't, and we carefully had to monitor her blood pressure and heart rate, but finally the moment came. We had the most beautiful little grandson in the whole world. The first time I saw his little head and tiny body will be a lasting memory. He was wonderful. Jen and Justin named him Lane Robert Mangum after the late rodeo rider Lane Frost and after Lane's Grandpa Robert. We were now grandparents and it was fantastic!

When we brought Jennifer home, she still wasn't feeling well and still fighting high blood pressure. One night Justin gave us a call saying Jen had a terrible headache and for us to come over. When we got there, Jen was completely out of her head. We called Keith Chambers, a paramedic in town and friend, and he came over; but for some reason he couldn't read her blood pressure. I was very afraid. It was not that long ago that my brother's wife had delivered her baby, and one week later she developed a severe headache that turned into an aneurysm and we lost her. It was a long night, but Jen did get better and her blood pressure problems finally eased.

Sweety had to share me with Bruiser, and now there was Lane. I showed Lane to Sweety. He looked at the tiny baby, but stood a distance back. Sweety had never seen such a small human. I think Lane scared Sweety. I wanted Sweety to get used to seeing Lane. I took Lane on several walks with me, holding him in my arms. The deer all stayed back some. I liked that they seemed to understand that Lane was precious cargo. Sweety licked little Lane's hand. He was so gentle. I could see in his big brown eyes that he could be trusted.

We had a wonderful Christmas. Having a baby in the family again was so much fun. Shopping for baby things felt so good. We dressed Lane in the cutest little Bronco outfits. The entire Hurd family were huge Bronco Football fans. We decorated for Christmas more than we had in years. Having a little baby around again was the beginning of big changes in our family. Robert and I spent our weekends playing with Lane. We tried to get out and take walks, but we were enjoying Lane so much that almost everything else wasn't as important. Sweety still was important, but even he took second place when it came to Lane.

It was the week before Christmas when the rutting season ended. Sweety had been in several battles with other bucks that had come through our area looking for does. He walked in one day with his face pretty bloody. At first I couldn't tell what was wrong. I was relieved when I saw it was only his ear that had been cut. He was bleeding badly though, so I did my first doctoring job on him. I cleaned his ear and poured peroxide on the wound and used some Neosporin. In a week the wound had healed perfectly. His front left shoulder also seemed tender, and I noticed he walked with a slight limp. I would rub the shoulder and hope it helped him some. I was glad the rutting season was over. Every year strange bucks came through, and some were really large. Sweety did not like these unwelcomed visitors in his yard and would quickly make the guest uncomfortable. I didn't want them around either, so both Robert and I would try and chase them out of our yard.

One day I was holding baby Lane while taking a walk when a small, young fawn just walked up to us. It was a little doe, and I'd never seen her before, but all of a sudden there she was with Lane and me. When I say, she was with us, I mean standing so close I could pet the little thing. She was clinging to us. I looked for a mother, but she was all alone. I did not want the responsibility of taking care of another fawn, but she sure wanted me to take her in. I'm not made of stone, although at times I wish I were. I wanted to turn my back on some animals and walk away. Then maybe I wouldn't hurt so much later. So many people seem to be able to just say let nature take its course. She's lost her mother, she'll probably die, and that's that. But, even though I believed she had to make it in the wild, I still would do my best to see that she survived. She was orphaned. We named her "Orphan." Then I got a breakthough —a pretty amazing break. Instead of her finding

Lane and me.

a mother, she got adopted by none other than my Sweety. He took right to her. He bathed her, and he protected her from the other deer. He would stand back and make sure she got to eat something before he or any other animal that might have been close did. Orphan followed him like he was her daddy, and

maybe he was. I was grateful and welcomed his responsibility for her well being. It was another thing Sweety did to make me love him more.

Orphan and me.

Baby Sweety Painting by Karen Hurd.

Chapter 14

Antler Hunt

It was the morning of January 23rd as I watched Sweety casually climb down off of Burton Smith's hill and leap over our wooden railed fence. Something was really wrong, and I was not ready as it was way too early, way too early. Sweety no longer looked like that magnificent buck that he was. He looked like a doe with two large holes in his beautiful head. Sweety's antlers were gone; not just one, both were gone. He had never lost them this early before, and usually when he lost one it would take days for the other to drop. I was sick. It was snowing pretty hard, and I had to go to work. There was no way I could go and hunt for them that morning. Working that day was no fun. I wanted out of the office in the worst way. I was praying that no one would find his antlers. I was afraid he may have dropped them both in someone's yard. That was a long day. I drove pretty fast up to my house, as I had to get out in those mountains as fast as I

Sweety missing antlers.

could. When I walked through the door Robert had our binoculars out and our boots and coats laying on the couch. He was also hoping we could find them because he knew how much I loved Sweety, and he also loved Sweety. Well, we hiked and hiked and we searched and searched, but nothing. Every afternoon, if we could get away, we looked for Sweety's antlers. Sundays we spent searching, trudging through deep snow, freezing our bottoms off. It is hard work walking through deep snow, but we did it over and over again, hoping we would find them. Coyotes followed us. I was really tired of seeing them so close behind me, walking in my trail; but I was desperate now and losing hope of ever finding Sweety's antlers. I was at the point where the coyotes didn't bother me as much as never finding those two beautiful antlers.

It was late March, on a Sunday, when Robert and I prepared for another day in the mountains. It was a beautiful day. The sky was so blue, not a cloud anywhere. I'm not sure how far we walked, but it was at least five or six miles and we were getting pretty tired. We ran into Sweety, his gang, and little Orphan on our hike. This was common though. We stopped and played with them awhile, and I was wishing Sweety could tell me where his antlers were. I would have given anything if he could talk. Then, as we were dropping off of a hillside into a meadow, Robert said he could see a large antler. In that second I also saw it. Well, the race was on. I moved pretty fast in that deep snow – fast, but graceful I wasn't. I knew whose antler that was, and I knew I wanted it. Even though I knew Robert would give it to me, I had to be the one to touch it first. So as I approached the horn lying there in the deep snow, I went sailing right over it. Robert didn't know whether to worry that I was hurt or to laugh at my clumsiness. He laughed as he picked up Sweety's antler and I pulled myself out of the deep snow. I had landed on my wrist and was worried I had cracked it. I wiggled it around and knew I'd survive. I was so thrilled to see Sweety's antler that I didn't care if I was injured. As I collected myself from all the excitement, I began looking for the other one. My prayers were answered! Right underneath a large pine tree, about twenty five feet away, was the other beautiful antler. Robert just stood still and watched me run. He knew to stay out of my way for fear that instead of a wrist I might break my neck. Sweety's antlers were and are my diamonds. I had found my lost treasure. I kissed them. I hugged them. On the way back home, as we walked by Sweety, I held the antlers up high and said "Sweety, look what I found." Sweety didn't seem all that impressed, but I was on Cloud Nine. I couldn't wait to get home and call my daughter to let her know of my find. I couldn't wait to tell Don Cardin I'd found them. Robert was happy too. We both were ready to rest.

Chapter 15

Bears

Lane brought so much happiness into our home. We watched him crawl, watched him pull his little self up, and then finally watched him take his first steps. I thought being a mother was the greatest thing, but being a grandparent sure runs a close second. I heard Lane speak his first word, which was "ball." He must have known then that he was going to love to play football, soccer, baseball, catch, anything that involved a ball. Saturday night was always our night with Lane. Jen and Justin would get some time alone, and Robert and I would look forward to the weekends. We often kept him during the week too, anytime the kids needed us.

Summer was always busy. The deer were gone, and the bears and marmots returned. We had gotten familiar with several bears and could recognize them from year to year. One bear (a very large female with reddish colored hair) had

Mama Bear

been in our area for several years. Needless to say we grew attached to her, as she seemed to have survived several traumas in her life. One year she had been hit by a car. Her whole right hip and right thigh were ripped open, and she was the mother of three cubs at the time. We knew that it was wrong to feed the bears, but this was a very bad summer for this bear family. The mother was in desperate need of help. Her cubs were thin also. I'm not sure, but I think after the hit by the car she stopped producing milk. We were guilty of throwing out our scraps for her and her babies. One night I went to let my dog out to go to the bathroom and, when I turned on the light, I had four bears stretched out on their backs with their feet in positions that made them look dead. It scared me to death. They looked dead. I thought I'd killed the whole family. Poor Robert! I started screaming, he jumped out of bed, and he ran into the living room. He too at first thought they were dead. I guess it was getting close to their hibernation and let me tell you, when they sleep, they sleep! It was like trying to wake the dead. Mama bear seemed to be healing, and we prayed she'd make it through the winter.

I'd like to tell you one more story about her that happened earlier. She once was tranquilized when she was seen way up in a tree by the Division of Wildlife officer. She had been raiding a campground. My husband ran to a local motel and borrowed several mattresses, because if she were to fall out of that tree she would most likely be killed. I was at work, and I was crying. I didn't want anyone to bother her, and the whole town was standing below the tree the entire day. That poor bear was terrified. After the wildlife officer tranquilized her, she fell and landed on a branch, but this was a blessing for her. The people waited, the officer waited, and when she woke she stayed in the tree until her audience all left. Then she returned to the wild. I was proud of Robert for making the effort to try to protect her if she fell. One thing that was a success from the event; she seemed to stay away from town. I know we were wrong in caring for her and getting involved with bears. I know. I know that just the heartache alone isn't worth it anymore. We did learn from all the wrong we did, but I also know one bear family survived a summer that I'm sure they wouldn't have without a little help.

The same summer that the mama bear was hit by the car, we also had a very young mother bear with two cubs running around. This bear seemed very young, too young to be a mother. I didn't know then what tragic moments were waiting for her, and how I would look at bears in a different way from then on. Early one morning, my husband had driven by a neighbor's yard and found a half eaten bear cub. He notified Phil Mason, who came and picked up the tiny baby. Phil told us that it was common for male bears to eat the young in order to get the female back in heat. This seemed so awful and we felt it probably was one of the young mother's cubs because of its size. Later that afternoon, as I drove into our driveway and got out of my car, I heard a lot of squealing in our backyard. I ran and got Robert, and we both went out to see what was making the noise. This was one sight I wished I'd never seen. If I had had a gun it would have been the first time I'd shot a bear. About twenty-five feet away was a very golden bear with dark-colored legs. It had a baby bear in its mouth and claws. The mother bear was crying so loudly it sounded like someone screaming. She was lying on her belly reaching one paw out as far as she could to try to reach for her young cub. I ran into the house and called Phil Mason. I told him what was happening and could we shoot the male bear. Phil said, "No Karen, this is nature." Nothing could be done but to let nature take its course. Watching that mother bear reaching for her partially eaten baby is a memory that will stay with me forever. We called the male bear "Killer," and every time we saw him we made him as unwelcome as we could. One late night we heard a commotion out in our yard and went to see what was going on. Our big old mama bear had torn into Killer. She was absolutely vicious. She was twice his size. I'm not sure of the damage she did to him that night, but I thanked her for running him away from our yard. We saw Killer once or twice after that, but he never came back to our yard.

This was a good lesson for us to learn about bears. We looked at them a little differently from then on, and I never got attached to any of them again. This also was the last summer the big mama bear would be around. We never knew what happened to her, and that is probably for the best. I think her cubs made it through the winter, because the next summer I'm pretty sure we had the three running together. Yes, they were trash bears (bears that eat trash), and I'm not sure what future they ended up having. I'm sure I contributed to their bad behavior and I am sorry for that. However, I'd like to say in defense of people and bears, that we have always had bears as long as I can remember in Lake City. As a kid, when I walked to town from my grandmother's house, on several different occasions we saw a bear cross the street. Also, while walking to the school bus in the early mornings, there were many times us kids spotted a bear in someone's yard. Bears in Lake City are not uncommon. We hardly ever heard of them breaking into people's houses like we do today. Back then, we had an open pit dump where trash was available to the bears. I believe this kept them from being so desperate for food. Since the closed containers have been put in at the landfill, more bears are getting into trouble than ever before. This is only my opinion, but something both Robert and I have witnessed over time. We get blamed for attracting bears with our bird feeders, yet I always had bird feeders. Robert and I built our feeders where it was impossible for a bear to get to them. I think the dump provided for a lot of scavengers. It was easy food for them, so that was where they spent most of their time.

Mama bear and her three cubs.

Chapter 16

Sly Gets Hurt

Sweety had come in that summer by August. I'm not sure why he had come down so early, but I was always waiting on him. He was beautiful in his velvet antlers. They looked so thick and monstrous. Beauty also was a giant this year. Both he and Sweety seemed to be the best of buddies. Sly hadn't come down yet, and that bothered me, because he was always running with Sweety. An older buck, which we had known for years and called" Star," had joined Sweety and Beauty. Star was an old Roman nose timberline buck. Robert said that bucks that had a Roman nose like Star usually came from the high mountain areas. Star was old when he arrived. He must have been eight or nine back then. Sweety and the other bucks always showed him the same respect they had shown Bruiser. Star was a cranky old thing, and I believe he had an injured right shoulder because he always walked with a limp. That injury probably was the reason he came out of the mountains. Star had a star on his forehead, which is how he earned his name.

Sly after he had been hurt.

One morning, as I went out in my backyard, I found a huge amount of blood on our rocks. There was so much blood it looked like someone had been butchered. Robert and I searched the area but found nothing. The next morning we woke to the sound of heavy footsteps walking on our porch. I thought it was Sweety, so I got up to give him a treat. However, looking through the window of our front door was a buck with his face completely covered in blood. I could see that his velvet antlers had been ripped or completely cut off from his head. I knew who he was in an instant – it was Sly. I ran out to him and he just stood there waiting for me. He was weak and hurting. I fed him some carrots and grabbed some bird seed to see if he would eat and get a look at his injured head. I didn't know if he'd been hit by a car or what had happened.

Sweety with Sly.

Robert and I both had heard of people trying to get velvet antlers for aphrodisiac, so my first thought was someone had stolen Sly's antlers. I knew I would have to try and doctor him, as flies were gathering heavily around his open wounds. All I could think of was peroxide and Neosporin. Sly never fought me at all when I was trying to doctor him. I used a wet rag and washed his face and wounds and poured the peroxide into the open holes. Next I took a tube of Neosporin and squeezed the gel into the wounds. While I was trying to help Sly, Robert noticed another young buck walk in with one velvet antler and the other gone. We immediately went in and called Phil Mason, thinking there could be someone out there doing this to the deer. Phil told me to keep watch, and if I noticed anyone in the area to call him. He, too, thought we could be right about the cause. He said to watch for maggots, and see if I could continue to keep Sly's head cleaned. I couldn't get close to the other buck, and it wasn't long before I didn't see him anymore. I hope he survived. The next three weeks I doctored Sly every single day and he finally healed. We bonded pretty closely.

Later I had a customer walk in the post office who told me a story of a buck that had gotten caught in his chain link fence and lost both antlers. Sly's mystery had been solved. I was glad that no human had done this to him. The other buck must have gotten his antler knocked off in some other way too. It was awful to think someone could do that to an animal. I was so happy to have been able to help Sly. Sly had always been such a loner. He was always so shy. For Sly to depend on me, like he had done, showed how far we had come together. Sly had found a buddy too, and that was Squirt. Oddly enough, before Sly's injury, he and Squirt were bitter enemies. Their becoming friends was hard to understand because a couple years before, Squirt, for no reason at all except being a bully, knocked Sly completely to the ground after he had dropped his antlers.

I couldn't believe what a bully Squirt was. He came from behind the large pine tree in our yard and hit Sly hard, right in his ribs. It was such a vicious hit, one that could have easily broken Sly's back; but, thank God, Sly got back up on his feet and seemed okay. I guess he never forgot, because a year later, when Squirt lost one antler and walked down off of the hill above our yard, Sly stood there waiting. It just took a second. We watched a head-on collision like two Mack trucks going at full speed crashing into one another. Squirt's one antler went flying off; and, although Sly only hit him once, it was enough to really shake Squirt up. I remember watching the antler fly in mid-air and disappear. It took us thirty minutes or more to find it. Crazy, it happened right in front of our eyes, yet we could not find it. Finally, way under a little bush, we found the antler imbedded deep in some branches. I believe Squirt was injured that day because from that moment on he had swelling beneath both his eyes. He would remain with this swelling the rest of his life. Oddly enough though, Sly and Squirt were now buddies. They remained together as Toughy and Handsome did. Squirt stood close to Sly as I doctored him and watched my every move. He seemed to understand what I was doing. Maybe their fighting was a way of earning respect for each other. All I knew was it sure seemed a deadly way of doing it. Sly would survive his trauma, yet he would go through this winter bullied by all the other bucks. Without his antlers he could not defend himself against them.

As close as Sweety and Beauty seemed to be, they also had a pretty bad argument that fall. While Sly was healing, and I was doctoring him, I had to give Sweety something to keep him from bugging us. Sweety did show jealousy. He wanted my full attention and didn't care much for other deer getting it, even if it was his brother. I would have to firmly tell Sweety on many different occasions, "No Sweety, be good, calm down." That Sweety, I loved him so much, and we went through so much together. I know he knew what I was saying. This animal was brilliant. He amazed me so many times. He was so gentle with me, but not with others. I saw his strength when he and Beauty had their first battle. Oh it was bad. It was fast and, thank God, I moved fast. I was thankful I had a shed that I could jump in. Like lightning striking, both Sweety and Beauty locked antlers and were throwing and shoving each other completely across my yard and back. I knew they both were about the same size and strength. Their necks were both bent back so far I was sure one would be killed. I was scared to death. Who would come out of this and survive?

I knew I couldn't distract them. If I did, I might cause their death. This battle lasted forever. Or at least it seemed like it. I was shaking and crying and I was praying Sweety would not be hurt. I could deal with Beauty being the loser, but not Sweety. Beauty, in a hunter's eyes, had the perfect set of antlers. They matched beautifully and were as tall and thick as Sweety's. This fight was equal. Their muscles rippled, the sounds they made were horrible grunting sounds. I stood paralyzed; there was nothing I could do. The fight finally ended and I'm not sure why. Maybe they realized no one was going to come out a winner. One of the tines on Sweety's antler had been broken and Beauty had a cut that was bleeding on his face and shoulder. They stood apart for some time. Then, like nothing had happened, they began licking each other's faces as if to say they were sorry. The fighting was over, and the friendship seemed stronger than ever.

Sweety with Beauty.

Chapter 17

Painting

I had begun painting a lot, since being around wildlife inspired me to try and paint them. My father, Larry Pavich, was a well-known artist in Lake City. He painted wildlife and scenery, but he also loved painting old mining camps. He was absolutely fantastic in drawing cartoons. When I was small, I would sit and draw with him for hours. Those were some of my best memories with my dad. After he passed away, I painted a mural for the town on the brick siding of the store where we kids grew up. The mural was a copy of a painting my dad had done of Uncompahgre Peak. I dedicated it to his memory, and a golden plaque was hung in his honor. After several years, the mural chipped away and it was eventually covered by white paint. Since then, I have pushed and pushed myself to become a better artist. I have studied artists like Carl Brenders, Robert Bateman, and John Seerey Lester. These artists' works take my breath away. Carl Brenders' animals look like you can reach out and run your fingers through the fur. Every strand of hair looks so real. I have never had any formal training by a teacher, but just looking and studying their paintings has helped me a lot. I once was blessed to have a conversation with Carl Brenders that touched my life forever. My goal is to one day paint as good as he does. That is a high goal, as he did tell me I would need to do nothing but paint and should not try and hold on to another job. I believe he's right, because to get as good as he is, I know it will take most of my time and dedication.

Before I started painting wildlife, I had painted hundreds if not thousands of butterflies that could be hung in yards. Robert and I spent hours and hours cutting and lathing the bodies of the butterflies. Then I would paint them and we would glue them together. Robert's mom would hang them in her front yard,

Sweety - my favorite painting.

which was downtown, and the tourists bought them for years. The next thing I started to paint was pet rocks. First it was people's dogs and cats, then deer, rabbits, raccoons, and bears. The rocks were a lot of fun and not quite as much work. Painting rocks helped us as much as painting the butterflies and taught me a lot about painting animals. Trying to make a rock look like someone's dog or pet wasn't always easy, but it sure felt good when I saw a tear of joy from someone because they thought it looked like their pet. Usually it was a pet that had passed away. I still paint rocks.

One of the first paintings I ever really worked on was my beautiful Sweety. Again and again, through the years I've painted Sweety. As with the rocks, I'm sure there will be more paintings of Sweety and all of the animals that have touched my life in some way. Painting is therapy for me, and to be known as a wildlife artist is a dream of mine. I wonder, if I had never known and loved Sweety like I did, would I have ever attempted to try and paint like I try to do now. Even when trying to write his story, he was an inspiration in my life, and he left an imprint on my heart forever. I always connected Sweety to my dad. I'm not sure why. Every time Sweety was missing I would pray to God for his return, but I also prayed to my dad to bring Sweety home and make sure he was all right. I wish I could tell you how many times I said a prayer to my dad and then looked out my window to see Sweety standing there. I even asked Sweety, "Are you the reincarnation of my dad?" I had moments that I actually felt he might be. Crazy as it might sound. I still think it might have been possible.

My first painting of Sweety.

Chapter 18

Jen Has Health Problems

It was in October of 2000 when both Robert and I noticed our daughter was having health issues. She had lost a lot of weight. She was eating, yet she seemed to never be satisfied and her mood swings were way more apparent than ever before. She also seemed considerably tired. One afternoon she and Lane came over and spent the afternoon with me. I had the day off, so as I played with Lane and visited with Jen, I noticed the huge amount of water she was drinking. I asked her why she was so thirsty, and she said she didn't know but she felt she couldn't get enough water. I made her make an appointment at our local medical center. I kept Lane while she went for her appointment. About an hour passed when I received a phone call from Jennifer and she was crying very hard. She told me the nurse said she had developed diabetes. He was going to give her pills and hope that it would control her sugar levels. This absolutely put us in shock. She had never been sick before, except for normal colds and things like that. She hardly had ever been hurt. Once she ran her little 4-wheeler into our parked truck and cut her finger, and she had a bike wreck once, but nothing ever was serious.

Justin, Jennifer and Lane.

In that instant everything changed. Her life would never be the same from that moment on. The pills weren't working, and we ended up in the emergency room at the Gunnison hospital. Her doctor, who had delivered Lane, was there and knew Jennifer well. Her blood sugars were over 800. The doctor felt she could go into a coma and immediately made her start taking insulin shots. Jen was diagnosed as a Type One diabetic, not a type two as previously thought. Her doctor told her, "Whatever you do, don't get pregnant." He knew she and Justin wanted one more child. Until she had her sugars at a safe level, he didn't want her to even consider pregnancy. Pregnancy was our last thought. I just wanted to see my daughter well. I had never been so worried in my life. Getting the right amount of insulin was a nightmare. Trying to figure out the dosage for each meal, fighting lows, or not getting her blood sugar down — it was insane. Her stomach looked like someone had taken a bat and beat her with it. Being her mom I almost always was able to fix what hurt her or make things better, but this time I couldn't. Watching her beautiful eyes fill with tears when she hurt herself with a needle was heart wrenching. Cooking took on a whole new role. I'd tried to help her with the meals. Not just her eating habits had to change, but all of ours had to change. We couldn't tempt her, and it was wrong to eat foods in front of her that could make her sick. Life changed and we had to change with it. Jen's health meant more than anything.

We had a good Christmas. It was the first Christmas that I didn't make Christmas candy. I tried hard to think of the healthiest dishes I could make. We shared all our leftover food with the deer, birds, and squirrels. Sweety seemed to like the sweet potatoes and the homemade rolls. Instead of any of us gaining extra weight over the holidays, our animal friends would. We all laughed about that. It was good to see Jen laugh. My Christmas wishes were that Jen would get better, to keep all my family healthy and safe, and, of course, keep Sweety safe too.

January came and I prayed that 2001 would be a great year. "Please God, make my daughter healthy again." Well, what started the year was my daughter going to the medical center because she wasn't feeling well and knocking on our side door at the post office to give me the news we were not supposed to get. I opened the door to see my daughter with these huge scared eyes looking at me. She choked out the words, "Mom, I'm pregnant." I just took several steps backward, not knowing what to do. Having another grandchild was wonderful, but her doctor's one request, "Please Jen do not get pregnant," sounded like sirens going off in my head. It was definite that Jen was pregnant and due in September. There was no going back. I just told myself that God doesn't make mistakes. I told Jen the same. There is a reason for everything. I strongly believe that. We were fortunate to have each other. Together we could get through anything.

I spent some quiet moments with Sweety and talked and cried to him. I didn't want Jen to see my fears, so I let Sweety see them instead. I think he knew I was going through something.

I hated that I couldn't give Sweety the attention he was accustomed too. He didn't demand my attention like before; he came in for meals, but would leave with the others. When Jen had good days, I tried to find time to spend with Sweety. I'd give him a special treat to assure him I loved him. One day I had a real difficult day and Sweety was lying in the back of my yard. I was worn out and not in a good emotional state. I walked over to Sweety. He was so used to me that my going over and sitting next to him was nothing unusual. Most deer would not allow this, but I walked over talking to him and crying. I sat next to this dear deer, he just leaned his beautiful head on my lap, let me scratch his ears, and listened to me cry. He didn't expect an apple or a carrot, just a hug, and I needed one too. It comforted me when he would look at me with those big brown eyes like he understood and could see my pain. I told him the whole story. He was my friend, maybe one of my best friends. No, not maybe, Sweety was my best friend, other than my family. I could trust him with anything, and he was there for me when I needed him. He licked my arm as if to say he loved me. This was a special moment between us, and one that I will hold forever in my heart.

Jennifer would have both good and bad days, but all in all she kept her blood sugar levels at a safe zone through most of the pregnancy. With Lane she had suffered high blood pressure, but with this pregnancy, at least so far, we hadn't had to deal with that problem. Spring was here, and one early morning I woke to find one of Sweety's antlers lying on our sidewalk. This was such a thrill, and to me a blessing, because I knew my getting out and hunting for them when they dropped would be difficult. I picked up his gorgeous antler and kissed it. I even loved the smell of antlers. They had been rubbed on aspen trees, and they always had a good scent. That same morning, about an hour later, Sweety walked in looking a little lop-sided. He did not like that and would shake his head, jump sideways, and hang his head to one side. He was just half goofy acting. I felt sorry for him. His antlers were his weapons, and they were magnificent weapons. I ran in and got him an apple, carrot, and a cookie. He was depressed and I wanted him to feel better. I offered him the treats, but as I did, I gently touched his remaining antler. All of a sudden I had it in my hands and was holding it while Sweety looked up as if to thank me for him not being lop-sided anymore. I felt awful and began to cry because I thought I might have hurt him. I would never hurt him. It really tore me up, but I was so thankful I had the matching set. These were my diamonds and a part of my best friend. I knew I'd treasure them forever. Sweety forgave me, or rather he thanked me. He never acted angry at all. Another bite of apple always fixed everything.

One morning my phone rang, and it was a surprise to hear Phil Mason, our local DOW officer, asking me for a favor. He started out by saying he knew how much I loved animals and how I had saved Sweety and Sly. He wondered if I might help save two more orphaned fawns. It was an honor to hear this from him. He said a mother doe had been hit and killed on the highway, and her two fawns needed to be found and would I help look for them. Phil Mason trusting me to do this meant more to me than words can say. He said, "If anyone can save them Karen, I believe you can." I searched the area over and over for nearly two weeks. Neighbors said they would call if the two orphaned fawns were seen. I walked miles and miles in search of the babies, but could never find them. I finally gave up and prayed they had been adopted by another doe, as we had seen this done several times. One day Phil walked in the office and thanked me for all my effort. I hated letting him down and letting the fawns down. I told Phil how much it meant to me that he had called me to take care of those two fawns. I thanked him and said I would help anytime he ever needed me. He said there was no one else he would have considered, as he knew I'd do all I could to help them. I didn't know that day that it would be our last conversation. I didn't know then that in a couple of months life for Sweety, Phil's wife, and the entire United States of America would be turned upside down and changed forever.

Chapter 19

Heartbreak for Everyone

It was September 3, 2001, my sister Cindy's birthday. Cindy and I weren't but two years apart in age. Cindy was killed in a car accident when I was twelve years old. Our parents divorced when we were very young, and Cindy played a huge part in my life. She was mama and daddy, big sister and friend. Losing her was something I've never gotten over and never understood why God thought he needed her more than I needed her. She always stayed on my mind. I always wished she could have seen my daughter and Lane, met my husband, and seen what a great family I had. Growing up, never having our mom and dad hardly ever with us, we were so lucky to have each other. I miss her everyday and especially on her birthday.

Robert and I had gone into Gunnison that day and we were eating at a Chinese restaurant. I got up to go into the restroom to wash my hands, and when I closed the door it swung back open. I closed it again. Well, it swung back open. I remember saying "Cindy are you in here with me." It was a strange moment. It was around four or five in the afternoon when this happened. On our way home, I thought about it several times. It had left me feeling uneasy. We got home and still I felt jittery. I was worried and maybe a little scared. I told Robert about the swinging door, and he didn't say much. Robert knew I'm half spooky anyway, so he thought it was probably best to ignore me. I felt funny though, and worried. The next morning Robert went to

Phil Mason, our beloved Game Warden.

work, but shortly afterwards he was back. He walked through our front door and he was pale as a ghost. He said, "Karen something horrible has happened." I could see that it was something really bad by the way he looked. I tried to brace myself against the wall. I was so afraid of what he was going to tell me. He was crying as the words, "Phil Mason was killed last night" came from his lips. I went to my knees saying, "Oh God, no, please no." He said, "Phil was killed while driving a tractor moving those huge rolled bales of hay, and one rolled on him killing him instantly." All I could think about was his wife Edna. She worshipped Phil. How was she? My heart broke for her. She loved Phil so much. We all loved Phil. The entire town loved Phil. Some might have had issues with him, yet everyone loved him.

Phil's funeral was like no funeral I had ever seen. It was held at our Community Center, which is one of the largest buildings in Lake City. It was so crowded that the building could not hold everyone. People were standing outside, lines and lines of people. I don't know how many were there, but I know almost the entire town of Lake City was there with several hundred more from around the state and even further. Saying goodbye to this wonderful man was so hard. Edna was lost. What do you say to someone who just lost everything? I could and would cry with her, hold her, and promise I would be there for her. Nothing would bring Phil back. I wanted him back too. He was a friend, and he understood me and the way I was with animals. No one could take his place. Lake City would never be the same.

Sometimes in your life you feel like the sky is falling or the world is ending. Edna was feeling like that. There was a part of me feeling the same way. We didn't know that in a few more days the world would be feeling like that. When it pours, it floods. That horrible morning, watching the television and trying to understand what I was seeing. The entire world at that same instant was in disbelief over what was happening right before our eyes. We were helpless. We were frightened, terrified, the entire nation was in mourning. September 11th, not one of us will ever forget that date. That day we watched the Twin Towers fall to the ground, the Pentagon bombed, the airplanes falling out of the sky. The world was in tears. Heartbreak would devour us; eat us alive.

Trying to cope with the loss of Phil was so hard. Now we had to cope with the loss of thousands more. Edna, Lake City, and the nation – it was the darkest time of our lives. What else can be said? Life changed in an instant and not one of us had the power to change it back. We took one step ahead of the other one. We had to rebuild our lives and move forward. We had no choice. Love conquers all; we joined hands. Together we combined our strengths. The U.S.A.

became one. Our flag waved proudly, and determination set in to each and everyone's heart to bring down the ones who had tried to destroy our lives.

I felt so sorry for Edna. She hadn't had time to mourn Phil and the last thing she needed to deal with was all that was happening. Life sometimes is far from fair. I knew I had lost a dear friend and soon another "deer" friend would be showing up. I wanted to see Sweety. I needed to see Sweety. I wondered how he was. I prayed he had made it through the summer without anything bad happening to him. I wasn't prepared though for the changes that were about to take place. Sweety and I would never be together the way we once were.

People talk, and for some reason some like to see others hurt. I fell victim to some of their talk. It seems that some of them hated the fact I had been playing with my deer friends. I knew there were laws that we were not to feed them, and I knew there were fears of wasting disease, though none of our deer herds ever had that problem. The wasting disease problem magnified, and all you heard about was how they were killing hundreds of animals because one case of the disease had appeared in an area. The healthy deer were killed along with the ones believed to be carrying the disease. I read where 300 elk were killed because it was believed the sickness was in the herd, and later it was never found. I don't know the details. It seemed so extreme to go to such measures. I was just so saddened to read all the stories about so many animals being put down. I was thankful that the disease had never shown its ugly face here.

All of a sudden we had new Division of Wildlife officers going to the town's people and demanding their feeders be removed. Fines were being issued. I heard comments on how Phil was too nice, and that big changes were coming. We were told how terrible we were for helping the deer in the winter months. In the Riverside area, where we lived, we had the best herd, the most beautiful, the most talked about; yet we were accused of causing them harm. How was I going to explain this to Sweety? How was I going to turn my back on him when he walked in my yard for his apple? My heart wasn't just breaking, it was crumbling. I was falling completely apart. I loved Sweety like I'd never loved another animal in my life. I loved all my animals so much, but Sweety was a huge part of my world. Other than my family, he was my world. We had just gone through the sadness of losing Phil Mason, then we had to come to grips with the horror of September 11, 2001, and now I really didn't have any strength left. I sure wasn't strong enough to turn away my best friend.

Sweety loved me no matter what I looked like!

Chapter 20

Shaylee

One bright star shined on our family, though. How thankful we all were on September 19th, when Shaylee Rae Mangum came into our lives. The worst of times and the best of times; the loss of lives and the welcoming of new lives. Shaylee was a shining little star. She lit up our world when everything seemed so black and dark. Jen handled the pregnancy better than she had with Lane. She kept the diabetes in control through most of her pregnancy. Her doctor suggested a C-Section instead of normal delivery. He felt this would make everything easier on her. It certainly made it easier on all of us. However, there were about twenty-four hours after Shaylee was born, when she had to be closely watched because of the insulin her mother had to take. Shaylee was nine pounds, she was a chunk, and she had a head full of black hair. What a cutie, and the best distraction we could have had. Jen was worn out and pretty sore, but still she was doing well.

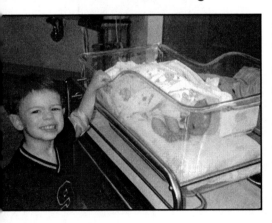

Everyone was happy except her big brother "Laner Bob" (his nickname), who wasn't exactly thrilled. Lane would look at Shaylee and have the funniest expression on his face. You could see he wasn't all that crazy about all the attention that little thing was getting. This creature had invaded his life, and he no longer was the center of all of our attention. Poor little guy; he was not a happy one. The day we were bringing Shaylee home, Laner didn't want us to. We all laughed when he whispered, "Do we have to take her home with us?" His expression will stay in my mind forever. I smile and laugh every time I think of Lane and that day. There were good

memories even when everything else seemed so bad. We tried hard to convince him how wonderful it was going to be to have a sister. Yet all Lane saw was that she cried, messed her diapers, and got the attention that was once his.

We all made it back home and got the new member of our family settled in her little room. I took some time off work to help Jen until she was feeling better. Jen had both Lane's and Shaylee's rooms fixed up so cute. She could decorate far better than her mother. They were so cozy and had Disney characters on the walls. I loved walking into their rooms because they instantly made you feel happy. My family made me happy. We were blessed and, at that time in our lives, we needed to know just how lucky we all were and not take things for granted. Treasure every day and treasure every one you love. Everything else in our lives was unsettled, and it was the same for Lake City and the world. We had a lot of "new" to get used to. Change was never something I accepted well. Change was my enemy. Change scared me. I had to accept change, but I was fighting it. I knew that it would cause me a lot of heartache, and I felt I was hurting enough over all that had already happened. One step forward, but I kept taking fifty back. It was a hard time for me because I knew I hadn't the power to get yesterday back, and I had to come to terms with what was going to happen and accept it.

We had a new, wonderful member added to our family. We were lucky and blessed; while so many others had their lives torn apart. I was angry with myself for being so sad at times. How could I explain to anyone that, even with all that was happening in the world, I was worried about the future of a deer, a wild animal – not a pet like a dog or cat – a mule deer? Completely crazy.

Chapter 21

Unwanted Winter

Winter seemed to be coming sooner than usual, yet the snow wasn't piling up because the temperatures were still warm. A few deer were coming out of the mountains, and I was waiting on Sweety and Sly. I didn't know what I was going to do, because Sweety spent ninety percent of the winter in my yard. He had a favorite spot where he laid. He even knew where the bedroom window was where I slept; and, often if I slept-in, he would come over to that window and knock his antlers gently on it. This would make Robert crazy! He just knew Sweety was going to break one of our windows. We had a big bay window. I worried so many times that Sweety would break that window. He wouldn't just use his antlers for attention. He also would knock with his foot. If I could no longer care for Sweety like I had for so many years, I feared the damage he might cause. I envisioned broken windows and a completely torn up yard. What was I going to do? How would I explain to him I couldn't help him or Sly anymore? Sweety thought he was family. How do you turn away family? They would never understand why I didn't seem to love them anymore. Yes, I know they are not human, but tell "our" deer that!

They were wild animals, and now I would get in trouble for taking care of them. Actually their being "wild animals" was a joke. My dogs were meaner to me then Sweety ever was. Talk about cry and being sick to my stomach. For the first time ever I wondered if it would be better if a hunter shot Sweety rather than watch him starve. My thoughts were killing me. I know myself pretty well, and I knew how much I loved both Sweety and Sly. I had to come up with some sort of plan.

The loss of Phil left the town for a short period without any Division of Wildlife officers. I always loved and respected the Division of Wildlife. Now

I feared them. I wondered if I could tell them about Sweety, and if they would understand and let me continue taking care of him. I had read many articles about people in other states being granted this wish by the local Division of Wildlife. I read how people in other areas of the country could feed and keep fawns and even tie ribbons on them to protect them from hunters. Darn, I talked to so many people from other states at my work, and they had deer feeders in their yards; they bought corn and fed all year long. What really blew my mind about this practice is that they lived in warm temperatures where food was plentiful year round unless there was a drought.

Here in Colorado, and especially on the Western Slope, our winters are usually severe, and food is far from plentiful. Our deer have to be extra tough and extra smart to survive. I've seen them in neck deep trying to paw and wade their small bodies through the huge amounts of snow. I've seen hundreds of dead bodies scattered about. I'll never forget driving on U.S. Highway 50 and passing stack after stack of dead deer bodies piled high after dying from starvation. I've seen grown men cry after seeing the loss of lives suffered in some of our harder winters. Hunters, who might shoot a deer or elk for food themselves, but who never wanted to see them die from starvation. How in the world would I, as much as I loved Sweety, let him go hungry? I worried that my future could be behind bars, and I'd never really done all that many bad things in my life. I didn't drink. I got drunk once and was so sick I swore I'd never do that again, and I never did. I smoked pot a few times, but I didn't like it because it made me tired and hungry, so I didn't do that anymore. I was never all that wild. I made a few mistakes, but I knew right from wrong and I didn't want to go down certain paths. I watched my mom's life fall apart, and I wanted more than that in my life. My husband had a new name for me. I was now a "dirty deer feeder." We laughed about it, but the truth was that if Sweety came into my yard and I went out to give him an apple, I would be a criminal. I would be breaking the law. It was a thought that killed me. I never thought I'd be on the wrong side of the law.

Several of the townspeople came into my office and asked me what I was going to do about Sweety since Phil had died. I would instantly feel the tears start to fall, and a painful and choking feeling would invade my stomach. I could see some of the people were very concerned, while others had smirks on their faces. They seemed to find some sort of enjoyment in my misery. I decided quickly that Sweety and Sly would have to become my secret, and my talking about them to others would have to end. I was blessed with a few friends whom I could cry to and trust; but overall I saw a narrowing down of friends, and it hurt me more than I can say. Most of my life, women had been my best friends, but now it seemed this was changing. Many of my women friends had opinions on what I needed to do, and that was basically to not have anything to do with Sweety or Sly. I guess they didn't want to see me get in trouble, but I began hearing talk from one or another on how I'd better stop taking care of Sweety and how wrong I was. I even began hearing I'd better stop caring for the marmots that lived in our yard in the rocks. I was quietly falling apart and scared to death. My heart was broken.

I missed Phil Mason so much. He never looked at me as a criminal. I knew if I had a friend who was in my position I'd be trying to figure out every way possible to assure her. Sweety and Sly would be taken care of. Yes, they were deer, but they were like my puppies, and although they were considered wild, to me they were the most gentle, wonderful creatures I had ever known in my life. I cried every night. I prayed on my knees to God for guidance on what to do. I waited for an answer, as I waited for Sweety and Sly to come home for the winter. I just had a few people now, other than my family, who I could talk to. Don Cardin was now one of my closest friends. He was a quiet man, a very educated man, who had spent his life studying fish and wildlife. He had even once considered becoming a Division of Wildlife officer. Thank God that didn't happen or I wouldn't have had him as a friend at that time of my life.

Don loved the elk and the mule deer that roamed and lived on the ranch that he took care of. One huge blessing, for me at least, was I could tell someone about my fears and they could offer support, instead of ridiculing me. Don would just say be careful, watch what I was doing; but he accepted and understood I loved Sweety, and that taking care of him was important to me.

Another blessing was that there were some of my neighbors who for years had taken care of the deer in our area. They would become vital in the next few winters if I was going to be able to visit and spend time with Sweety. They were two elderly women, who I had known most of my life. They knew all about Sweety and loved him too. Thank the Dear Lord above for the friends that Sweety had also made. I told them my fears and they said, "Honey, when

Sweety and Sly come down this winter you can come up to our little valley and be with them." This offer was absolutely priceless. Sweety was smart. No doubt about it. I could train Sweety to meet me there instead of in my yard. The little valley was private and hidden away from everything. If I could just teach Sweety and Sly to go there, then maybe I could continue taking care of my pets. Yes, to me they belonged to me. Sweety and Sly were mine. Convincing me otherwise was pointless. I was so thankful for my family and the few friends I still had who understood and accepted the way I felt. Without them I might have lost my mind because of the worry I was putting myself through.

Chapter 22

Being With Sweety

It was on the morning of the 18th of October, when we heard something fall or hit hard on our deck. The loud noise startled both Robert and me. Our first thought was maybe a bear was on the deck and hitting at our window. The bears were getting ready for winter and were more aggressive as they searched for food to prepare for their long hibernation. We'd never had many problems with bears like we had heard others in town had. Once a bear ripped a hole in a cage where we were keeping two mini-lop rabbits and tipped the cage over. And once a small bear got into one of our sheds and Robert had to open the door and let it out. This morning, however, we had a lot of movement and noise on our porch. As I ran to the kitchen from the bedroom, all I could see were two white bottoms, eight legs, and one set of very large antlers. I knew who it was. Sweety had pulled one of our baskets of pansies off the railing of our deck, and he and Orphan were sharing the flowers. We always saved the flowers in our pots for him and waited to watch as he climbed up on our porch to eat every last bloom and stem. I wanted to run out as I'd always done before. I was yelling at Robert in excitement, saying, "Sweety's home and Orphan's with him." I searched like crazy for an apple or carrot to give to them as a welcome home gift.

Sweety knocking at my door.

Every year, for quite a few years, Sweety had been a five by five. He was magnificent. Each year, his antlers just grew thicker and thicker and also longer. He was so beautiful to me. He turned and looked through our large bay kitchen window, and when he saw me his tail stood straight up and wagged. I went straight out to him. I could not stop myself. I prayed as I walked out the door that no one would see me and report me as I fed Sweety and Orphan an apple. I petted both of them; but while I told them how happy I was to see them, I cried. Sweety leaned close to me and nuzzled my shoulder with his wide wet nose. Little Orphan just stood there letting me pet and love both of them. I hadn't seen Sweety or Orphan since last May, and you would have thought that after that much time passing there would be a little fear from such animals. I was intimidated by Sweety's size. I knew how powerful and strong he was, and to walk right up to him after such a long spell apart probably wasn't smart, but those huge brown eyes of his and the wag of his tail always was my sign that he wanted me to come close to him.

I scratched him under his neck. He loved that. I had pulled ticks off him many times, so he always liked me to scratch him there. His temperament was much like a horse. I could brush his back with my hands and run them across his huge body, but I never feared he'd kick me like I feared a horse might. I trusted Sweety more than I'd trusted all the horses I'd ever been around. All of these years together he had never shown one threatening act toward me. Horses left me with memories of broken ribs, scars on my side from being kicked, and sprained ankles that seemed to never heal. Sweety had never hurt me at all. Just my heart was hurting, and he wasn't the cause of that. Love, it rules me. My heart rules me. Boy, was I one big mess. Sweety was home, and now I had to try and get him away from our yard and train him to meet me up in the valley. Tough love is something I'm not good at, but I knew it was the only way I could be with him. I still could not believe I now would be considered a criminal and I would have to sneak around like I was having a torrid affair. And, all the time, all I would be doing was trying to be with Sweety.

The only thing I had going for me at that time was that the Division of Wildlife officers were busy with hunting season and didn't know me from Adam. They were busy sending new officers into our area, trying to fill Phil Mason's boots. That was one job I felt strongly could not be done successfully. In my eyes, Phil could not be replaced. What an awful feeling, though, being glad they had so many other commitments. That they couldn't worry about a dirty deer feeder in the area. I had to get a plan together and find a strategy to train Sweety and his buddies to meet me up on the mountain. But, could I? I couldn't even train my dogs to lead correctly! They took me on walks; I never took them. My ''Rotten weilers'' pulled me in every direction. Rotten they were. I spoiled everything. I was not a boss, but I had a lot of bosses.

However, I had to take command of Sweety's survival because I really doubted he would be able to make it on his own if the winter got severe. I doubted many deer in our area would survive without some handout, because for years they had been taken care of, not just me, but by half of our neighborhood. I knew they needed to learn to survive out there without everyone's help or my help. They had survived before I came along. But I believe the deer in Lake City, for how long the Lord only knows, always had a handout from the townspeople. I was not the only dirty deer feeder in Lake City. Probably more than half of us were guilty. Lake City had the most beautiful deer, so I know we helped them survive. They were healthy and breathtakingly beautiful. Lake City is not full of rich people either; and to help the animals survive, we all dug in our pockets. We didn't ask for help, but felt in our hearts we were helping. We went without some things to assure that the deer survived; and easy to feed these animals, it wasn't. Robert and I were always month-to-month with our money. I didn't have diamonds or fancy clothes. I'd go without, not thinking twice about it, though, if I knew Sweety was taken care of. In trying to help my daughter and her family, and with Robert and my own expenses, money was always short. No one could take care of all the deer, but we could take care of a few. I had a bag

Sweety came in every fall and helped himself to all our potted plants.

in our safe that each year I stuck some money in. The bag had Sweety's name on it and that money would be all I could use for him. I struggled to get that bag full by the fall when he came back. It was hard to come up with extra money; but it was worth it. I loved Sweety, and he was worth it.

The same morning that Sweety and Orphan walked in, it wasn't an hour later before Sly showed up with Beauty, Squirt, Little King, and several others. They must have all chosen to come down together. I ran out to Sly and gave them all an apple. They all ate out of my hands now. It seemed that if Sweety trusted me, they all did. Whatever Sweety did, they followed him. I liked that they trusted me. It was a gift from God to me. Being around such magnificent wonderful animals that would come to me rather than run away from me was a pretty neat feeling. What an experience. Not many could do what I could do with these animals. Robert could pet Sweety, but not even he could get too close to Sweety, nothing like I could. Sweety accepted Robert, but he still stayed a distance from him and only once in awhile did Sweety choose to let Robert feed him or pet him. If I was around and told Sweety it was okay, then Sweety would let Robert feed him or a friend of mine feed him. Robert never could get close to Sly. He worked hard to get close to Squirt because Squirt was his favorite. Squirt seemed to like Robert also, but mainly it was me that the deer seemed to have no fear of and trusted.

Squirt

Sweety and me. He liked his head scratched.

Chapter 23

Close Calls

I'll never forget the time when we had some carpenters working on our house and one badly wanted to pet and feed Sweety. He begged me to let him try. So I agreed, cut up an apple, and went and called Sweety to come over. The young man stood by my side and reached out his hand next to mine as Sweety approached to take the apple from me. At the last moment, I gave the apple to the carpenter, but as Sweety began to eat the apple he all of a sudden jumped back on his hind legs and snorted fiercely. The young man would not get to feed Sweety. It must have been his scent or something. Sweety knew my scent and knew this man was not me. I laughed. It made me feel good because I didn't want Sweety to trust just anyone; and he had proved to me that he did not trust just anyone. But now I had to try and get Sweety out of my yard. I wondered and worried if I would lose his trust. I had to get all of them out of my yard, and I had to start now. Robert was stern with me. He raised his voice many times, telling me I could no longer feed Sweety in our yard and that I had to get him and the rest up to the valley. I wonder how many tears I cried over all of this, probably thousands.

I began stuffing my jacket with bags of grain, and I filled my pockets with apples. I tried to beat the deer in the afternoons and meet them as they headed my way. I showed Sweety the grain and would toss apples as I walked toward the valley, hoping to make a trail. I already had them following me, so if I had grain with me I had them not only following me but nearly chasing me. I got them into the valley and I made it a routine. It took time and it took effort, but I began feeling it could be done and that Sweety and I could still be together.

I put myself in danger by not realizing what lay ahead of me. The valley was a private place and a wild place, which not only the deer seemed to visit. As dusk fell one evening I headed up to take a little grain and see if I could find Sweety. Robert was on the computer and didn't feel like going with me. It was still fall and bears were still in the area. I snuck up the mountain and into the valley and called to Sweety and a couple of other deer. Sweety seemed a little nervous. As I stood under a large spruce tree, he did come to take an apple and he ate some grain. Little King came along with Sly and about three or four other deer. I was calm and they seemed to be calm, but all of a sudden, from somewhere, there were loud barking and snorting sounds that screamed harshly at us. Sweety, Little King, Sly, the other deer, and I were trying to go in every direction, and yet none of us knew where to go. What in the world was making those awful sounds and where were they coming from? I was lucky the deer didn't run right over me. I was trembling. My knees were shaking like crazy. I had the feeling that I had to look above my head, because I knew the scary awful sounds were coming from above. Oh my goodness, the biggest black bear I'd ever seen was hanging from a branch, snorting and threatening us with all he had. I thought deer could smell things like that. I was pale as a ghost when I got back to the house, still shaking. I learned a lesson that day, though. Always look in the trees,

I learned to always look up.

especially before you stand below one. I laugh about it now, but for awhile there I had the biggest bruise on my bottom from hitting a rock pretty hard as I scattered in panic with the deer. That day left a physical mark on me that seemed to last forever, and a memory I will never forget.

My next close call came around Christmas time. The snow was getting deeper and it was a cold December. I was ready for January, hoping for a new year and a better year. I had gotten the deer familiar with their new feeding area, though it was sure tough on me. Packing grain and apples through snow and freezing temperatures was no fun. The bears were gone and I was glad about that. Coyotes and bobcats were the only predators we usually had around Lake City, and I pretty much had lost my fear of them. We hiked so often and had run into these animals so many times that I was getting used to them. They had always run away from us before, so I felt safe. We had a pretty large white coyote in the area. He had been around for years. Robert once had his gun sighted in on him and was going to kill him, when I stopped him from shooting the animal. I hated killing anything, and yet I hated what I knew the coyotes were doing to the young fawns and the older deer. They were killing machines and we had too many. The coyote population had grown enormous since trapping was outlawed and so many new hunting rules had come about. I didn't believe in trapping, as I felt it was cruel; but these animals seem to populate more than most. Some of these new rules really didn't make much sense. Ranchers were losing baby calves to coyotes that waited as the mother cows were birthing. I heard awful stories of how coyotes killed their prey. Anyway, some things you can't do anything about. I knew this all too well and had to live and accept certain things I felt were ridiculous.

Well, back to my close call. I trudged through the snow, took out the grain, and fed Sweety, Sly, Orphan and the others what I had packed up to them. Then I played with Sweety for awhile. I noticed the deer kept looking off into the trees, so I knew there must be something out there. I watched until I saw the big white coyote walking through the trees and even walking past several deer. I didn't think much of it and continued petting and talking to Sweety. My hands were getting really cold, so I hurried my visit, kissed Sweety on his nose, and left the valley.

I climbed down off the hill and then looked back to see if Sweety was following me, as sometimes he would try and I would have to chase him back. I thought I heard something following me and was startled when I noticed the large white coyote standing on the hillside. I was probably about twenty feet downhill from him. I waved my hands and yelled for him to go away. This must have just made him mad. He came running down that hill straight for me. It all happened so fast, I couldn't even find a stick to throw at him. I started to run when I saw a buck, which I had named Pretty Boy, come from out of nowhere with his head straight down and his antlers pointed in the coyote's direction. The tables had turned fast! I no longer was in danger, but a yelping coyote was running for his life as Pretty Boy chased him out of the area. I hadn't even tried to bond with Pretty Boy, and yet that day he might have saved my life. It was another imprint on my heart that would only make me love the deer more. Again I walked into the house, pale as a ghost with shaking hands and knees. Robert lectured me and told me that I was going to get killed. I knew he was right, but nothing was going to stop me from taking care of Sweety.

The town had a new game warden. He was a young man, and I wanted to like him. However my first impression wasn't all that good. I knew it would be hard to accept this man and find the respect for him that I had felt for the late Phil Mason. His approach to many of the local people was that things were going to change. "The new guy was in town." When he walked into a room, just the way he carried himself made you feel his presence, and the feeling was uncomfortable. I think what really got to me more than anything was when the rumors flew that he said he would not run his job like Phil Mason ran things. He didn't even know Phil, and for him to judge how Phil ran things really got to me. My opinion of the young man was formed and tainted from that moment on and, being honest with myself, I knew I would be on the wrong side of this man from the start. In my eyes he could not replace Phil, nor understand the way I felt about Sweety. The young game warden and I would never see eye to eye. Maybe he was right and I was completely wrong, but Sweety was one beautiful, healthy animal and I believe, no matter what was said, I played a large role in Sweety's survival and how healthy Sweety was.

January and February were bitter-cold months. One evening in February my husband and I had gone to Gunnison to get groceries and on our way home, late at night about five miles out of town, we noticed a large buck running straight down the highway at full speed, heading straight for us. We pulled to the side of the road, and as the buck came closer, running as fast as his legs could carry him, I noticed that it was Pretty Boy. He passed us without acknowledging that we were even there. We wondered and worried about what had caused Pretty Boy to do this in such bitter cold weather. All we could think of was maybe a mountain lion had been chasing him and, because of the deep snow, he chose the highway to try and get away from the lion. A week passed and no sign of Pretty Boy. I was sure he was dead. He must have run for miles, and the cold weather and running hard like that was surely a deadly combination. By the end of the week though, here walked Pretty Boy into my yard. He was thinner by a lot and held his head high in the air. I knew something was wrong. I was glad to see him, yet I knew he was sick. He had chased a coyote away from me, and now what could I do for him. I called my local vet, and he said unless I could bring Pretty Boy to him or get the Division of Wildlife involved there was nothing he could do. He did say though that after what we had witnessed the buck had probably developed pneumonia. I had felt

that all along. I remembered that when I cared for six Rottweiler puppies with pneumonia, I held their little heads up high for thirty nights so they could breathe. I lost two, but saved the other four, and developed ulcers during that time. I wanted to go and hold Pretty Boy's head up for him. I owed him! I did try and get him to eat, but he just refused to pull his head down. The next morning I found Pretty Boy dead. I'll never forget what he did for me and how I wished I could have helped him. I cried. I hated the fact I couldn't save him. He was such a pretty boy. I felt I let him down.

Pretty Boy

82

Chapter 24

I Lost My Sly

That winter Robert took a lot of pictures. He had gotten really good at photography. The valley was so pretty, and Robert enjoyed taking pictures where there were no houses. He never liked taking pictures in our yard, so this year he took a lot of pictures for me of Sweety and the rest of the crew in the valley. We didn't spend a lot of time there, but when we did we got some beautiful pictures, and we enjoyed ourselves so much. We could sit in the valley on the rocks, and the deer would lie down close by us. It was so relaxing, not only for Robert and me, but the deer seemed to like and enjoy our company as well.

Spring was on its way. I was always ready for spring. I'd gotten Sweety through another winter. Thank you, God. I thanked him so many times. I believed that if God saw that I was hurting Sweety that I wouldn't have been given the chance to care for him. Sweety had survived and was doing well, so in my head I told myself God felt I was doing the right thing.

One morning Robert called me to come and look at a buck that had fallen through the ice over at the local sewer ponds. He said the game warden had thrown a large buck's body into the landfill, but the antlers were cut off and he couldn't recognize who it was. Oh how I hated hearing that a buck was dead. That news always sent chills up and down my spine. I drug myself to the dump with Robert, dreading to see the animal and praying that I would not know who it was. I wished I could have, at that moment, never loved these deer. Why did I allow myself to fall in love with these animals? Life was hard enough. The heartbreak was more than I could stand or take.

Sly, one of my babies was gone.

Sly lay there in all the trash. Oh Lord! I fell against Robert and burst into tears. One of my babies was gone. I crawled down into the garbage and held the blood covered head in my arms and thought I was going to die. I sobbed and sobbed. I wanted to take him home and bury him, but Robert said we couldn't remove him from the dump. It would be noticed, and we could get in trouble. I wanted to bury him; I felt half crazy. He did not belong in the dump. Leaving him there was tearing me apart, and the thought that he had drowned just killed me. My sister had drowned, and now one of my babies had drowned. I begged Robert to get George, Robert's brother, to help us get Sly, because George had the machinery and we could bury Sly. Robert pulled me away and nearly had to carry me to the truck. Oh God, how I hated leaving Sly, especially leaving him in the town's dump. Poor Robert! I was such a mess. I begged and begged and cried and cried for Robert to bring Sly home. That afternoon, late in the day, Robert came home with a large trash bag. He had taken Sly's head and brought it home, so at least we could bury a part of him in our yard. At least a part of my baby was home.

Robert dug a deep hole next to where we had buried Bronco, one of our dogs. I made a wooden cross, and we had a small funeral for our beloved Sly. I hate to

admit this, but sometimes when an animal dies I cry and hurt more than when some people die. That is an awful thing to admit, but it's the truth. Animals seem so innocent to me; and unless the person is a child, I'm stronger when older people die. Animals to me are like children. I took this death very hard, and I knew Sweety would also miss his brother. I hurt for Sly, myself, and for Sweety's loss also. It would take a while to get back on my feet and smile again. I was also angry at the young game warden who tossed Sly's body into the dump as if he were a piece of trash. I knew he didn't know that Sly was special, yet I was angry with him.

Chapter 25

Sweety's Missing

I sure didn't want spring to start this way. I could not understand why Sly had even gone over to the area of the sewer pond. What made him go over there, and why would he walk out on the thinning ice? When I saw Sweety, I wondered if he knew Sly was gone. I think he did, there was just something about the way he looked around as I fed him. It was like there was someone or something missing. He always had to share his food with Sly, but this time Sly wasn't there, trying to steal part of his apple. I cried as I talked to Sweety and told him about Sly. I hadn't thought about the thin ice and told Sweety to please don't go over that way. I hoped he understood me. Here I was, crying and talking to a deer, and I just wasn't crying I was bawling. Tears were pouring out of me. If someone would have seen me. I'm sure they would have thought I'd lost my mind.

Sweety seemed to take off earlier than usual that year, and this really worried me because I wasn't ready for him to leave. I began to panic over his being gone so early that spring and feared the worst. I knew where he loved to spend the summers, so I pleaded with Robert for us to hike up there and see if I could find Sweety. I'm lucky I'm still married! Robert has put up with a lot of my craziness over the deep love I felt for the deer and Sweety. I'm sure he felt that if he didn't agree to go look for Sweety, I would make his life miserable. I could read his mind, and he was right. I guarantee I would have made him miserable because I was.

Sweety spent the summers up in a beautiful valley on the land that Don Cardin watched over. I thought the world of Don, and I knew this land was posted and that people could not go on it without permission. I thought of calling Don and asking him if I could go and look for Sweety. I felt he would probably tell me I could, but yet I felt I was putting him in an awkward position. If he had to tell me no, it would be hard on him and me. I also knew not telling him could put me at risk of losing his friendship. I was going one way or the other though, with or without Don's permission. So without his permission was my choice, and I hoped he wouldn't catch me, so he wouldn't be put in any situation that would be difficult for him. I'd heard how hard he was on people who trespassed on his land. Don's friendship was so special to me, but I would risk it for Sweety.

We made our way to the valley. We could see deer grazing on the tall grasses. I instantly recognized several of them and some started walking toward me. I had cut up some apples and fed Trouble, Squirt, and a few of the others, but as of yet I could not find Sweety. I began calling for him as I stood among the other deer and the tall aspen trees. The sun was shining brightly on the hill above the valley. It was a beautiful day. Robert stood back and let me call Sweety's name, when he said, "Karen, here comes a deer running towards you." He told me to look on the skyline and I could see it. I looked up and, against the blue sky, I could see a deer running along the side of the hill and heading my way. It was Sweety, and he was running to me. I wished I had that on film, as it was a scene that caused Robert to shake his head in disbelief. To see such a large wild animal running to greet a human, just like a dog would, was pretty amazing. I hugged Sweety's neck. He was fine. He had just chosen to leave early. I left him in the valley. I left smiling. He loved it there and so did I. If I had my choice, I'd live there too. I'd give anything to own that valley. I wished the world could have seen Sweety running to me against the bright blue sky. What a beautiful sight. I can close my eyes today and still see him running to me. A memory that forever will stay with me. What a wonderful day.

Chapter 26

Gossip and Summer

The weather was getting warmer, so when I was at work at the post office I would open my window to get fresh air because the office seemed to get so hot. Right in front of my window was a parking lot. I noticed the new game warden driving up and getting out of his truck and walking in to get his mail. I heard him having a conversation with a local woman. Behind the mail boxes I stood listening, because I heard her saying she had information for him on people she knew were feeding the wildlife. I knew this woman well, and I watched her go to her car and grab a map. She stood with the young officer right in front of my opened window. I couldn't believe what I heard. She was giving him names and pointing her finger on the map at homes he needed to hit. He got out a pen and marked each place that she guided him to. I heard several names mentioned, including mine. I wondered what set this woman on this mission and what any of these people had ever done to her. I had considered her a friend for years. I believe everyone she was speaking of considered her a friend. I know she lost at least one friend that day.

It was two days later when I heard a knock on my door. Standing there was the new warden. I opened it and greeted him and asked him what I could do for him. He told me he wanted to check out my yard and look at my bird feeders. I went outside with him and let him go over my yard inch by inch. I was thankful Sweety had decided to leave early that year, because even though I'd stopped feeding him in my yard, he still would lay there some days for hours. Robert had made the best bear-proof feeders. Phil Mason had said he wished everyone would build feeders like ours. I told the young man that. Our feeders stood on top of seven-foot poles made of PVC pipe filled with cement. A bear could not climb or pull down our feeders. I painted the pipe to look like aspen trees, so that they looked pretty in our yard. He walked over to our burn barrels, which were empty, and I was thankful for that. For several years Robert and I, in both the spring and summer, had begun taking our trash to the dump to avoid having the bears tip them over. The game warden asked me to put up a rim around our feeders so bird seed couldn't spill and land on the ground and also to vacuum any spillage. A marmot walked up to the warden and stood and put his paws on his knee. I cringed, but the warden just laughed. I told him they'd been in my yard since we moved there and were very friendly. I agreed I would do what he asked, and then he left.

Robert got home, went and bought some copper siding, and built a small wall around our feeders. I vacuumed the seeds that had fallen. I continued to do what was asked of me the rest of the summer. I didn't mind his requests, as they were reasonable; but I resented who had sent him to my yard. I had no intentions of feeding the bears, and I wanted to respect the young warden, for he was only doing his job. I knew, though, he'd never understand the friendship I had with Sweety. My only concern was Sweety and a few of his followers. It was nearly summer now, and Mother Nature was seeing that Sweety was taken care of, so I could put my mind at ease for now. I had a difficult time being nice to the woman who had reported all of us after that. I try hard to smile and greet people the way I like to be treated. I had to grit my teeth and bite my tongue and try to make my mouth turn up to look like a smile every time she entered our office. That was so hard. I'm very much like my grandmother, "Moma Mick." I wanted to speak my mind in the worst way. She had turned in folks who were her customers for years. I know Moma Mick would have let her have it. I just pretended I had a sock in my mouth when she came around. I nearly choked on that sock many times.

Chapter 27

Moose and Mom

It was pretty normal that the marmots poked their little heads out of their winter dens by the end of March or early April. Just like the deer, they were very gentle and loving creatures. After hibernating all winter, and us not seeing each other, they still instantly knew me. I could talk and walk right up to most of them, and they would greet me as if they were happy to see me. I was always happy to see them. They were my sign that warmer weather was on its way – warmer weather that would be here to stay for awhile. I was always ready for that. Nothing felt better to me than the sun touching my skin. I couldn't lie out in it for long, but I love to work out in the yard and feel the warmth on my arms and face. The marmots would stretch their small bodies out on the rocks and sunbathe most of the days. We didn't have a dandelion in our yard. They were great at eating them. They were good watchdogs too. If anything approached, they would let out a whistle of warning. I loved them. I especially loved the way they bonded with each other.

Mama marmot grieved for a long time after losing Moose.

I'm not sure if they all mated with just one marmot forever, but I witnessed my Momma Marmot always with the big marmot that I had named Moose. These two were always together, building their dens, gathering grasses, and taking care of their young. Moose was trapped and moved by some of our neighbors along with several more of my marmots one year. I watched Momma Marmot mourn for weeks after Moose disappeared. She would rub and sniff each rock and cry a terrible moaning sound. She even quit eating for awhile. Robert and I searched and searched in hopes of finding where Moose might have been released in the hopes of bringing him back home, but to no avail. After Moose was no longer in our yard, it sure seemed the marmot population began to get out of control. He had (though we didn't like to see it) often killed the baby boys so as not to get too many in the same area. We had a lead marmot, pretty much like you'll see a lead bull elk or a lead buck. Until he was moved, Moose was the king in our yard. He ruled and controlled his harem.

Lane loved the marmots. He was just getting big enough to really enjoy them. He would giggle when they came to him and crawl on his lap. Shaylee was still too small to enjoy them. We all spent hours every summer watching and enjoying these animals. Some days after work, when I drove up in my car, the marmots actually ran out to greet me. They'd be standing on their little hind legs trying to jump into my arms. It was fun to come home to that kind of greeting. But I even had to be careful about taking care of the marmots, although all I ever really did was give them a carrot once in awhile, and they also loved peanut butter cookies. It wasn't like I fed them so much that a bear could walk in and get their food. The marmots cleaned up everything. A bear had a lot of competition in my yard. I'm not sure if it's against the law to feed the marmots, as they are of the squirrel family, but it felt like everything I once could do I could no longer do. In a way Robert and I felt forced to care for them, because we had plants we didn't want them to eat. A carrot would usually be sufficient food, and they would leave our plants alone. Even though we went to a lot of effort in planting plants that neither the deer nor the marmots liked, there were always some of our flowering plants that were tasty to some animals. I sure hated that what I used to love to do now seemed to be so wrong in everyone's eyes. Mentally,

it was tough. I felt at times like a bad person, and yet I knew if someone needed the shirt off my back I'd give it to them. If someone was hungry, I'd see they were fed. I'm not sure how I got on the "wrong side."

Chapter 28

Life

How did I get to this point in my life? That was a good question. All of my life I loved animals. My sister Linda also loves animals. I wonder if it has anything to do with what our lives were like growing up. I know it's common for people to love animals, but Linda and I have actually put animals before humans many times. Perhaps it was because growing up in a home that was pretty unsettled we lost trust in people. Maybe it was because when everything seemed so bad we found comfort in a pet, hugging a puppy, or petting a cat. I go back in my memories a lot and try to muddle through some of them to see if I can understand myself better.

Steve, Linda & Cindy

My folks divorced by the time I was three, but they had lived apart long before that. I've never seen a baby picture of myself. Crazy, but it bothers me. Three years old is the earliest I've seen. My mom told me it was because there was a house fire and the baby pictures got burned. I should accept that, but for some reason just my pictures got burned. There were baby pictures of my two sisters Linda and Cindy, and baby pictures of my big brother Steve.

We kids hardly ever lived with our parents, although I remember us all living with my mom in Gunnison, Colorado, for a short period. Mom had married a man I think all of us kids hated. He would put clothes pins on our cat's tail, and it hurt our cat enough that one day the cat never came home. He also would bring boxes, and I mean boxes, of dead rabbits home; and, as small as I was, he made me skin them. We seemed to live on rabbit stew and I just couldn't eat it, so I spent most of my time in the corner. He hated my sister Cindy. He beat her with a belt until she had welts all over her body. On Christmas or birthdays, he gave Cindy nothing – so that made all us kids refuse his gifts. I remember once on a picnic we had all gone on, he went out in the forest and started making these loud sounds like a bull or some kind of crazed animal. I had caught a frog and was bringing it home to keep, but when he made that sound it scared all of us so badly that we all went running frantically. We were all shaking, and when we reached the old truck and tried to get inside I went to check if my frog was okay. I had squeezed the little frog to death. I had never killed anything in my life. It was awful, and I hated that man more than ever. Mom finally left him.

Mom had such a drinking problem. She would go on binges and, for a week or two at a time, she would be so drunk she could hardly walk and would go without food for days. We couldn't get her out of bed and I remember the awful smells. Alcohol, throw up, and days without a shower. So many times I thought she was dead when she would pass out and we couldn't wake her. I remember her crossing a street in Gunnison right in front of the First National Bank, and I was so small and couldn't keep up with her. She was dragging me, and my knees were bleeding something awful. I remember someone coming out in the street and trying to help her and me.

My brother had gotten in a lot of battles with kids at school because mom had such a bad reputation with men and alcohol. It would scar my brother for life, and he never could forgive her. I wish I could say we had wonderful childhood memories, but I can't and I have to think real hard to find a happy memory. Seemed life was so unsettled, and we kids never knew what would happen next. Mom worked as a waitress in Gunnison; and when she was sober she did well. But, she could never seem to go more than a couple of weeks and she would be drunk again, lose her job, or fall out of another relationship.

My Grandfather, Daddy Frank and me.

Finally Mom's mom and dad, Moma Mick and Daddy Frank, came and got us kids and took us home to Lake City. How I loved the two of them. However, the relationship between my Mom and Daddy Frank was strained and unpleasant. They fought all the time. Daddy Frank wouldn't put up with Mom's drinking. Moma Mick told me she and Daddy Frank had to get married because she was pregnant with Mom, and she thought he held resentment towards Mom. It hurt their relationship, and she worried it was one of the reasons Mom had begun drinking. Moma Mick always protected Mom, and sometimes I wish she hadn't. Moma Mick's only son had been killed and all she had was mom; so I understood why she did it, but I'm sure it didn't really help. Mom would come in so drunk at times and Moma Mick would swear she was just sick. She babied Mom and Mom just took advantage of her. Daddy Frank would get mad, and we would have to listen to constant arguments between them. Some fights got physical and scared us a lot. I think I'd hide in a corner and hold my dog or cat and just pray that the fighting would stop. Alcohol had such an awful hold on Mom. I've seen and known a lot of alcoholics, but I'm not sure I've ever seen an alcoholic worse than my mother.

We would pour whiskey down the toilets and the kitchen sink every time we found a whiskey bottle. Mom would hide them everywhere. She would get to shaking so bad if she didn't have a drink that it would scare us so much that we would finally give in to her begging. Often we cried and pleaded with her to make a choice between drinking and us kids. I hate to admit what she chose. I know she loved us, but alcohol had such a grip on her that it was hard for any of us to understand.

Cindy and I ended up moving from Moma Mick's and Daddy Frank's to Mammy's. I can't remember why. Mammy ran Mike's Grocery. She had worked hard all her life. I believe raising Cindy and I put a lot of stress on her. Mammy and I never saw eye to eye, and in her eyes I never did anything right. I couldn't even walk through the door without her instantly telling me something was wrong with either my hair or the way I dressed. Dad one day pleaded with her to stop picking at me. I never quite understood why we had such a hard time, but a few years later I was told some things that answered some of my questions.

Alcohol not only hurt my mom, but once it nearly caused my dad to lose his life right in front of Cindy and me. Cindy, Beth, and I think a girlfriend named Laurie Brown, and I were all out playing in the ditch by the side of the highway near the grocery store. We'd been floating our Barbie dolls down the ditch when we heard yelling and screaming coming from inside the store. We started to go into the store, when Cindy and I saw our dad walking toward us with his stomach completely ripped open and blood everywhere. Daddy's chest and arms looked like he had been butchered. He walked outside and looked at us, and we were screaming. Daddy turned and headed up the stairs to where his bedroom was. I ran into the store. My Uncle Mickey walked past me and Mammy was standing in the kitchen with her jaw bleeding horribly and a huge hole in her face. I was crying, and Mammy told me that Uncle Mickey had stabbed her and Daddy with the butcher knife. I ran back outside to see my dad holding a rifle on my Uncle Mickey. Blood was pouring out of my dad. Mickey got in his truck, pulled out, and headed down the road. Daddy had his sights on him, but then he put the rifle down and cried out that he couldn't kill his brother.

Jim Ryan was a pilot who lived in Lake City and also ran a restaurant and bar across the street from the store. Jim Ryan saved my dad's life that day by flying him to the hospital in Gunnison. I'm not sure how Mammy got to the hospital, but someone took her. Uncle Mickey was banned from Lake City for the rest of his life. Mickey was drunk that day when he stabbed Mammy and Daddy. It seemed alcohol haunted the whole family.

Daddy Larry, Cindy and me.

My sister Cindy was killed in a car accident when I was twelve. The driver had been drinking. I think they all had been drinking. It was awful. Cindy was everything to me. I was told she broke her neck, but later read that she had drowned. Cindy was afraid of water. Today I still pray her neck was broken and that she did not drown. The night Cindy died I realized for the first time that my Dad and I had a problem. I needed him to just hold me. My sister had died. I needed him to be there for me. He called a friend to stay with me that night, while he slept with the woman he was living with at the time. It hurt me. I never stayed at his house again. After Cindy died, Dad stopped going to all my school functions, he stopped buying school clothes for me, and he stopped buying Christmas presents. I was only twelve. It all was very hard to understand.

In time I was finally told some things that gave answers to all my questions.

My Dad's wife and a friend told me Daddy never thought I was his child. I put together the many times my mom showed me a picture of another man she had known and loved. The sad thing to me is that I feel I have proof that both my mom and dad were wrong. God gave me a talent to paint. My dad was an artist. I wish today he could see how well I paint and draw. I took after him, yet he went to his grave believing I wasn't his child. So many years wasted. Dad was killed in a car accident. He was a great driver, so what happened to him was very ironic. Daddy had been drinking at a local bar in Lake City, got in his truck, and backed over an embankment. We think Daddy tried to jump out as he had done so many times when he drove loaders and caterpillars. On several occasions he said he had to jump to avoid being hurt or to save his life. This time, though, jumping out was what killed him. The truth though is alcohol is what killed him. Drinking and driving.

Mom shot herself once while drinking. Good thing she was a bad shot. After Dad died, she had been reading old love letters that he had written her years before. I could write a book on all the troubles my mom had. She loved animals just like her daughters did. I think they were a comfort to her also. One time my old dog "Spike" saved her life. She had passed out in the snow. I was walking home, and if it had not been for Spike, I would have never seen my mom. I called to him, but he would not come to me. I walked over to him and that was when I saw my mom lying in the deep snow. Spike saved her. Spike not only saved her, but once he saved my grandfather, Daddy Frank. Daddy Frank had gone into the mountains hunting for ore. He loved mining. He tripped and broke his ankle. Spike and another dog, Droopy, were with him. Spike left Daddy Frank and came all the way into town and to the house. He pawed on our door and barked. We knew there was something wrong. Spike would never leave Daddy Frank. Because of Spike, we went looking for him and found him. Spike was the one to thank. Spike was my dog, he was my companion. He went with me everywhere. He was very protective and nipped a few people, but he just loved me like crazy and I loved him.

I loved my cats, my dogs, and my horses. My happiest childhood memories were ones shared with them. They were always there when I was sad or lonely. I could count on my animals, when I couldn't count on my family. If an animal broke my heart, it was because it died or got sick. I couldn't say that about people. I was always afraid of the dark, and I can't tell you how many times my cat Coco and Spike would both jump up on my bed and lie beside me. After my sister died, I don't believe I'd have made it without these animals. I needed them and they needed me, and I think they kept me going. Losing Cindy was like losing both a mother and a father and my best friend. She looked after me and always took care of me. I wanted to die after she died. I was so lost. I had to keep going, though, because I needed to take care of my pets. Thank God for my pets. Guess that's how I got to where I am today. God blessed my life with animals.

What we experience in life is what builds our character. My mom's life was my greatest teacher. I learned from watching her. I knew I didn't want to live life the way she did. My Dad is the reason I became an artist. Maybe I was always trying to prove something to him, but it made me realize how much I enjoyed painting. Painting was a special gift that was God's way of answering my childhood questions. Mammy was hard on me. She told me on several occasions that I wasn't a Pavich. That was our last name. Besides painting, I love to write. I love to write songs. My daughter loves to write songs. And guess who else loved to write songs? Mammy! I was all Pavich. We probably didn't get along because we were too much alike. I truly believe that every experience I went through was valuable and had an answer for me that was needed.

In my greatest memories growing up, there's an animal in every one, or a creature of some kind. My first drawings were of animals, and they still are all I want to draw. I'm passionate about it. It thrills me to try and paint them and try to make them as beautiful as they are in real life. Without animals in my life, I wouldn't be me. I'd be lost. The only thing I can think of that has made me smile more than watching animals is watching my child and my grandchildren growing up. So I guess that's how I became what I became. A dirty deer feeder! I have to laugh about it. I have to laugh about a lot of things. I might as well laugh, because there's nothing I can do about it anyway.

Well now you know a little about me and why I am the way I am. I know that's no excuse for doing what was considered wrong – taking care of Sweety in the winter months, but I always felt a connection with my dad around Sweety. I said it before; I thought Sweety might have been a reincarnation of Dad. I had a friend in Sweety; I was happy when I was with Sweety; Sweety made me feel special. Sweety inspired me to paint, and he was my model so many times. We all have certain things that keep us going, that get us up in the morning, that make us smile and make us glad to be alive. Sweety just happened to be that certain thing for me. Sweety healed the hurt between my dad and me.

I went through a lot when I was growing up, some very painful times; but I think, other than my sister dying and my daughter having diabetes, what I was experiencing at this time of my life was nearly as hard. I was just thankful that Sweety made it through another winter. Now summer was here and I would try and enjoy it. I would put into God's hands how I would deal with the winters that lay ahead for Sweety and me.

My Family

97

Lane and Shaylee in our yard playing with the marmots.

Chapter 29

The Drought

Summer would be busy, just like always. Having Lane and Shaylee made everything seem a lot better. They helped both Robert and I feel young again. We got to watch them most weekends, so we always tried to plan something special for us to do together. We would toss Lane the ball and he caught it every time. He was quick and seemed to catch on to sports at an early age. He loved to watch the rodeo on television and also watched the monster truck shows. He learned all of the trucks' names and the names of the drivers. He'd spill them off his tongue so fast it would amaze anyone. Fast learner!

Shaylee was the sweetest little baby. She always had a smile for you. Robert and I loved being grandparents. We both wondered why we never had more children. I'm sure work was our reason. We never seemed to get ahead, and both of us worked hard. We wanted Jennifer to have what we never did, and one child was about all we could have. I hated her growing up without a sister or brother, but I guess that was the way it had to be.

We spent a lot of the warm evenings up at Lake San Cristobal. We loved to fish and have family picnics. Robert and I would also hike as often as we could. It was this summer that Lake City was having a severe drought. Everything was so dry that we had red flag warnings every day. Colorado had some terrible forest fires that year, and we had several small ones in our area. The town advised people to gather their valuables and put them somewhere safe. I put all of our favorite pictures away in a box. They were the

things that concerned me the most. I knew I couldn't replace them. We put them into fireproof storage for safety. I'd never seen the hills and meadows so dry. I worried about a forest fire and what Sweety would do in one. I wondered if he would be smart enough to get away from a disaster like that. I would look up at the area where I knew he loved to be in the summer and make sure I saw no signs of smoke. If I had seen smoke, I would have probably headed straight up the mountain side to see if I could find him and bring him home. Drowning and burning to death were two of the worst ways I could think of for anyone or anything to die. We were lucky, so very lucky that Lake City was spared that year.

Because of the dryness, I knew early on food would not be plentiful for the animals that winter. The field grasses hadn't grown tall and had turned so brown that I was sure the nutritional value was gone. Deer and elk, both, would have a tougher year because of the drought. I liked not having so much rain, but this summer I prayed for rain every day. I wanted the animals to have food. To try to provide for them was nearly impossible now. I'd gotten to take care of Sweety the last winter by pure luck, and I wasn't sure how long my luck was going to last. I didn't want to worry about Sweety in the summer months. Summer was my time to have a break. Worry I did though; every day praying for rain and praying for us not to have a forest fire.

Chapter 30

Don and
Hunting Season

I had done a lot of painting and was fortunate to sell several of my works that summer. I continued to paint round river rock, trying to make them look like animals. The most popular rocks I painted were of bears and fawns. They looked like they were lying down on the ground. They would look nearly real sometimes, and that made me feel good. I did a lot of pet memorials on rocks, trying to get the rock to look like the owner's pet. After a long day at work, to come home and pull out my paints and begin painting would relax me more than anything else. I'm not sure how many paintings I'd done of Sweety. I know several of his paintings are hanging on people's walls around town. He was getting famous and didn't even know it. Before I started a painting I always prayed to Dad to help me. It's so funny, but after Dad's death I leaned on him more than ever. Often I felt he was right there, helping with each stroke of the brush. He and I were closer now than we ever were while he was alive.

Bow and arrow season started in August; September would be muzzle loading; and then rifle season, which would last until December. I had pretty much stopped talking about Sweety except with my family. I knew I had to. Maybe if he wasn't talked about, people would forget he existed and I wouldn't draw attention to him or to myself. I began worrying in August and, as always, dreaded the months ahead. The only person I talked to other than my family was Don Cardin. Poor guy, I bet there were times he would have loved to shoot me. I told him several times, "I'll give you the gun." One of the reasons he got so much abuse from me was that I knew Sweety liked being on his land. I also knew Don was a hunting freak, and I also knew Don took other hunters out to hunt. I could not give him a break. I had worried about forest fires all summer and now I had hunting season facing me. It would pour on the pressure. I felt pretty sure that if Don killed one of my guys he could not face me. Don would come in and we would talk about several of the bucks running on his land. There was one that my daughter knew well, and she had named him Wiley. Don wanted that buck.

Wiley was a hunter's dream. Don nearly was foaming at the mouth for that buck. Oh well, too bad. I told him Jennifer loved that deer. No, he couldn't kill him or let his hunters kill him. I'd plead and beg, and Don would glare at me. How we remained friends is a mystery to me. I had heard from others that Don told several of his hunting buddies not to kill the town deer, as they were pets and that is not hunting. He should have shot me, but I am forever thankful for all he did to protect my Sweety and some of the others. I know he did not have to. It went against his nature and all he lived and loved to do. However, if Don wanted his mail and if he wanted to live in peace, there were certain things he had to do. I was thankful I could talk to him about Sweety and ask him to watch out for him. For some reason I felt I could trust Don. At least Don knew who Sweety was. He could recognize him from the others, which was hard for some

Wiley

people; but I'd shown Don so many pictures that he knew Sweety well. He knew Squirt too. He would bring photographs in of the deer he would see out on the ranch to show me. I would have my photographs, and we would together point out who was who. By the time we were done, Don learned that he couldn't hunt the deer in the pictures. I would say to him, "Guess you better hunt out by the cut off." The cut off was about twenty miles north of town. I don't think Don thought I was funny. I'd laugh and he would mumble something, and out the door he would go.

Chapter 31

Bad Sweety

When the shooting began again, the deer came down. Sweety led them into my yard, just like he had done every fall before. Same thing, again and again. I'd go out and hug him and was so happy to see him. He'd climb on my deck and eat every last bloom in my flower pots. He'd come to my front door and paw the door with his hooves. He was home and demanded my attention. Robert lectured me hard, and it was obvious he wasn't going to let up. I couldn't give anything to Sweety, even if he came to my yard. I began pulling our window shades down so Sweety could not see me through our windows. I hated doing this. It just killed me, but I had to do it. My teaching Sweety to go up to the valley would have to start all over. Some days I felt worn out and I didn't have the energy to climb to the valley, but I did it anyway and Sweety followed me.

I sure missed Sly. It wouldn't be the same without him. Beauty, Squirt, little King, Two Cute, and Trouble were the first to come into the yard after Sweety.

I wondered where Orphan was, but it was just a day or two later when she showed up. She was so small. She still looked like a fawn, but now she was about three years old. I wondered if she was ever going to grow up. Her growth had to be stunted from her being an orphan. Robert had a soft spot for her; so if she came in our yard, I'd catch Robert giving her something to eat. He'd say she just really got to him, and she was so sweet and seemed to need help more than any of the others. Even though he lectured me about feeding the deer, I never lectured back. Orphan was

Orphan

a sweetheart and a very tiny little girl. Sweety still liked her too, but he didn't have to help her get food anymore. She might have been small, but she was full of attitude; and she bullied her way to get what she wanted. I was glad to see she could be aggressive if she needed to be.

I dreaded and hated being back in the same situation all over again. Trying to take care of Sweety and his friends, and praying I wouldn't get caught. The stress was huge. I thought of quitting several times and told myself God would provide. I was fooling myself, though. I knew that, the way summer had gone, food wasn't going to be plentiful. I knew it just by looking at the deer that fall. They didn't look as good as they had in the years before. Sweety was still strong and beautiful, but some deer seemed thinner and more hungry than usual. There also seemed to be more deer down low, and that was the last thing I wanted. Taking care of Sweety and just a few others was very hard on my pocketbook. I'd had a lot of dental work done that year, and money was short. I'd have to really be careful about what I did. I knew I could only care for the few I had intended to take care for from the beginning. Robert lectured me on that too. He'd say, "Karen we cannot take care of all of them. There's no way." I knew he was right, but how I wished that the others that used to help with feeding would help again. I wasn't good at walking away from a hungry animal, but I would have to in order to be able to care for the ones that I had grown close to. I knew that when I lost Sweety I would stop trying to care for the deer. It was getting me down and causing me too much heartache.

The rutting season had begun, and with more deer in the area Sweety had more competition. I had seen him fight before. I'd witnessed several others fight also; there had been some pretty serious battles, but I never saw them kill each other. I knew that, as strong as they were, they could kill one another pretty easily; but I'd never witnessed it. I received a call from a neighbor one morning telling me he had watched two bucks fighting and that one of the bucks had died in the fight. He asked me if I could come down and look at the buck before he called the game warden, in case the dead buck was Sweety. I was babysitting Lane and Shaylee at the time, and I had never left them alone. I asked Lane if he could just sit and watch Shaylee in her playpen for me while I went down real quick to look at the buck. I said I would be right back. Lane said he would. I felt terrible leaving them alone, but I ran as fast as I could to where my neighbor told me to go. I instantly recognized the dead buck; I had called him "Crooked Horn" for several years. Crooked Horn used to run with me, and I was fond of him. He laid there lifeless in a ditch-like area against a small clump of ground. I was sick. I hated that he had been killed.

I ran back to the house as quickly as I could, and Shaylee and Lane sat there waiting. I hugged them both and said I was sorry I had left them, and then I told them it was Crooked Horn that had been killed. I called my neighbor and told him who it was, and that it wasn't Sweety. My neighbor said he took a picture of the buck that killed Crooked Horn and that he would bring it to me as soon as he got it developed, to see if I could tell which buck it was. It was a couple of days before my neighbor came in and showed me the picture at work. I hated seeing who I was seeing. I could tell my neighbor hated the animal in the picture, which made me hate telling him who it was. I whispered out Sweety's name. Yes, it was my Sweety. My neighbor had nothing kind to say about Sweety and that hurt, because I knew a whole different animal. He wasn't a vicious killer. I knew this year he was having a tougher time keeping his status in the herd. I believed he had to prove himself to the others and show them that he was still king. By killing one of them, he got his message heard. There were too many bucks that year in the area, and some were larger than Sweety. They were intruding on his territory, and he hadn't ever been pushed like he was being pushed this fall. He killed someone I knew he had befriended through the years,; I'm not sure why. I wished he would have fought one of the strange bucks rather than a friend. I couldn't change what happened though, and I hoped my neighbor could forgive Sweety in time. We didn't understand all that status stuff, and nature sometimes can be so cruel. I still loved Sweety, and when I saw him again he was as gentle as he had always been. I wished he could have told me why he did what he did. I had watched Sweety being so protective over Orphan and Sly. It was hard to believe he intentionally set out to kill anything.

Deer sparring and results after fight by Al Lutz.

Crooked Horn

After the fight.

Chapter 32

Sweety Protects Me

Seemed things were just going wrong for Sweety and me this winter. The one thing that I feared would happen, happened. One afternoon after I got off from work, I headed up the mountain to do my daily deed. The day seemed normal, and everything was going as planned. Sweety was waiting for me as I dropped down into the little valley. I would greet him with a kiss on his nose. He had the most awesome nose. Sweety had a beautiful nose. It was wide and strong and I must have kissed it a thousand times. Lots of deer have thin noses and that makes them not as strong looking. It was just a special trait of Sweety's, and it made his appearance more magnificent. Anyway, he and I and, as always, some of his buddies were in the valley together, and I pulled out the grain I had carried up for them and poured it on the ground for them to eat. Then the most dreadful sound came from above me. "Hey, what are you doing, Karen?" I wanted to die, oh dear I was so scared. I looked in the direction the voice was coming from. I knew who the voice belonged to, as it was familiar to me. I just said please, please don't tell anyone. The man who I knew really well just laughed. He said, "Caught you red handed girl." I couldn't speak because I was so close to tears. He said, "Is that Sweety?" I said yes. Then again I begged him not to tell. I told him it was the only way I could be with Sweety, and he told me not to worry. He wouldn't say a thing. I asked him what he doing here, as he was on private property; and he said he was just out hiking. He admired Sweety and the others, and said he'd do the same as me if he were in my shoes. I was so thankful, and he seemed to mean what he said. He patted me on the back, told me not to worry, and said to continue to take care of those deer; then he left. He and I never talked about that day again.

After that happened, I was more nervous and, I guess, more in a hurry than I normally had been. The hillside was slick, and there was quite a lot of snow on the ground. After I fed Sweety and was getting ready to leave, I tripped over a rock. I knew I was hurt. A very familiar pain hit me hard, and I knew I was in trouble.

Since I was child, my right shoulder would dislocate, and I would have to have someone put it back in its socket for me. I would instantly go into shock when my shoulder came out. The pain was horrible, and my shoulder hung several inches below where it should be. I knew this pain all too well, and I lay there on the cold ground not knowing what I was going to do. I yelled for Robert, hoping he would be outdoors and maybe he could hear me. I cried and I yelled for help. The deer had never seen me down like this. I scared all of the deer away except one. The entire herd left the valley, except my Sweety. I was down and couldn't get up because I had to reach around and grab my arm and pull it forward someway before I could even begin to get on my feet. Dealing with the terrible pain I was in and dealing with Sweety was something I feared might be the end of me. I wasn't sure what Sweety was doing; I could see he was upset. He snorted and walked back and forth for several minutes. I was in such pain that I couldn't do anything about Sweety's fear. He was scared and did not understand my lying there on the ground. The pain was so severe. I felt I could pass out or get sick to my stomach any minute. I had to think of a way to pull my arm back to my side. My yelling for help was useless, but I couldn't quit. Sweety would walk toward me, then he would back up. The cold air intensified and went right through me. I knew I was in the early stage of shock. I had begun shaking and couldn't stop. I was flat on my back, crying and shaking, and Sweety was as upset as I was, if not more.

For the first time ever I was terrified of Sweety. My lying there on the ground had made him extremely nervous. It was apparent by the snorting sounds he was making. I had to calm myself down. I quit yelling for help and started talking to Sweety. I said, "Sweety, I'm hurt and I've got to get on my feet." He walked right up to me and put his big nose on my stomach. I still hadn't pulled my arm around. It was totally over my head. I'm sure I looked pretty awful. Sweety stared at me, and I just kept talking to him saying, "Sweety, I've got to get up." He then picked up his right front leg and placed it on my other side. I was completely underneath him. He was standing over me. He looked like a monster. One swipe of those huge antlers and I would be done. I began to cry, but I kept talking to him and reaching to try to bring my hurt arm to where I could gain some control. I touched Sweety's leg, and when I did he slowly started moving back. I felt safe all of a sudden because his actions were slow and calm. I pulled my hurt arm to my side. It hurt so bad; I was in agony. I slowly began to sit up. As I did, I reached up to Sweety and leaned toward his front shoulder until I had enough leverage to get my knees beneath me and pull myself up on my feet. Sweety stood there without moving. I felt like I might pass out, but I knew I had to get to my house for help.

Burton Smith's house was below me, but he was gone. He had put my shoulder back in for me many times and had finally taught Robert how to put it back in place. That was the longest walk of my life. I was in shock, and the pain was terrific. I wasn't alone though. Sweety was right by my side. Step by step we walked down the hill, and if I stopped Sweety stopped. I leaned on him several times when I thought I might be blacking out. We made it to my yard and then to my front steps, still side by side. I kicked at the door and Robert heard my cries and came running to see what was wrong. I had to lie on our kitchen table and Robert put my arm back into its socket. Thank God, Burton had taught him how.

As fast as my shoulder went out, it went back in. I was close to being sick to my stomach and told Robert I had to go outside for air. Robert walked out with me. As we stood on the porch, Sweety went back and forth snorting like crazy. He acted like he was threatening Robert. I told Robert what Sweety had done for me and that maybe he better go back in the house. It was apparent that Sweety was upset and perhaps still worried and confused on what he and I had just gone through. The way Sweety acted toward Robert – I'd never seen him act that way before. Robert had no choice but to leave and go inside. I think Sweety had every intention of attacking him. His ears were back, and he made every threatening move he knew. I talked to Sweety until I had calmed him down. That day our bond had grown so much stronger, and I never thought that could have been possible. I loved him more now than ever. We went through something together that changed me forever. Sweety took care of me. We switched places, and this mule deer took charge and took care of me. Sweety got me up on my feet and down that mountain. He stayed with me the whole way. My precious Sweety! I knew he was special. I always connected him to my dad, maybe he was my dad. Was he reincarnated? Crazy thoughts, but they felt possible now. I knew I'd never look at Sweety in the same way as before. The fear I felt as he stood over me was absolutely terrifying. Then the love I felt from the experience we shared was absolutely overwhelming. A wild animal, yet he showed more love and concern for me than I could understand. Lately I felt like it was him and me against the world. Who could not protect an animal like this?

Robert couldn't believe the way Sweety acted that day. We talked about it several times. Sweety was special, and what happened that day between us would never be forgotten. From that day forward, Sweety received more treats, an extra apple, a couple more carrots, and ten times more kisses on his nose. I sure didn't need to love him any more than I already did, but I did.

Spring was on its way again, and all my deer seemed to have survived except for Crooked Horn. Robert would correct me when he heard me say "my deer." I knew they weren't "mine." That was just a figure of speech. Sweety was mine, though! I claimed him and had full ownership in my head. How I wished I did own him. Yet I knew in my heart he loved his freedom, and I would never want to put him in a pen, even if the Division of Wildlife gave him to me. I always wanted to protect him. I knew that even though he wasn't mine, we had a strong connection and bond between us. He made the choice to spend time with me, and that meant more to me than having him in a cage and forcing him to be with me. I found his beautiful antlers that fall. I was only missing one of his antlers in all of our years together. His antlers told his story – how he had grown from such a sweet little guy to an absolute beauty. I think his antlers also proved how healthy an animal he was. He must have had the right nutrition to grow such awesome antlers. I could take pride in that, as I felt sure I played a part in his being healthy.

Every night before going to bed, I went into my living room and got down on my knees and said my prayers. I prayed for everyone I loved and for the entire world. I ended my prayers with a special one for Sweety. I knew he was leaving me again to play in the mountains another summer. I thanked God for letting me care for him in the winter, and I prayed I would see him again as soon as the fall colors began to shine like sunlight lying upon our mountains and valleys. I also prayed that no one would ever hunt Sweety. The thought of him being killed by a hunter scared me. I would have to take full blame because he trusted me and had lost a lot of his natural fear of humans.

Saying goodbye each spring was never easy, and I would always try and keep him with me as long as I could. Yet, when I saw the bright new green leaves popping out from the branches of the aspen trees, I knew Sweety would soon be gone. What a winter we had together – precious memories that would forever stay with me. I had a very special friendship that was as rare as gold. I was so fortunate to be blessed like this.

Chapter 33

Another Loss

It was early June and Sweety had been gone for over a month. I loved visiting with Don Cardin, as I usually would learn something from him when we had the chance to talk. I could tell that something seemed wrong as I watched Don get out of his truck and walk into our office that day. When he looked at me he shook his head. As Don opened the front door to where my working station was, I just said, "What's wrong Don?" I knew he had bad news for me; I knew by the expression on his face. I could feel a sickness in the pit of my stomach. Don said I needed to drive out past San Juan Ranch and, once again, look at a large buck that had been hit by a car. I know Don was as worried as I was that maybe it was Sweety. He said all he knew was that it was a large buck. I thanked him for telling me, and he left. Beth told me to do my books and leave early so I could look at the animal before the State Highway Department removed the carcass. I called Robert at work and told him what Don had said and asked him if he would meet me at the house and drive me out to where the accident was. I didn't want to go alone. If Sweety had been killed, I wasn't sure how I was going to handle it.

Robert picked me up and we drove out to where Don told me to go. The buck was lying just off the highway. His body was large. I got out of the truck and went over to him with shaky knees. Mule deer change so much from fall to summer. Their gray coats turn red and all their winter scars disappear. Without their antlers and with the new growth it's sometimes hard to identify which animal you're looking at. The buck's head was bloody; and, even though I strongly felt it wasn't Sweety because it had a much darker patch of fur on its forehead, I feared it might be Beauty. Cars were passing by, and people were staring at me looking at the dead buck. I was crying because I knew it was someone I knew. Robert said, "Honey, we have to get out of here, you're drawing attention." I left feeling strongly that the buck was my dancing Beauty, but I wasn't a hundred percent sure. I could not bury him in my yard. I had to walk away and wait to see which buck would not return next fall.

I called Don and told him I wasn't sure who the buck was but felt positive it wasn't Sweety. I told him it might be Beauty. He said he knew it was just a very large buck and hated seeing it dead. He complained about how fast people drove in that area. I agreed with him; everyone seemed to speed on that stretch of highway. Often elk and deer were seen close to the road there. Slower speeds would save a lot of lives, and more signs were needed. Shortly after the accident, the State Highway Department put up several new wildlife crossing signs. I was glad to see them. Now I would have to wait and see if Beauty came back to dance for me.

Chapter 34

The Love of Summer

Anyone who lives in Lake City works their tails off in the summers. The businesses have about four good months to make enough money to get through another year. During the winter months snowmobiling brings in some revenue, but not a whole lot. Many of the restaurants and shops where tourists find unique gifts open up in the summer. Lake City is a wonderful tourist attraction. Fishing is great, and mountain biking, hiking, and hunting bring people from all over the United States and even further. The Fourth of July is a huge event and a fun family time for everyone. Many retirees have second homes in Lake City; and they come up here to get away from the heat and traffic, and to have a relaxing summer. It's a pretty wonderful and beautiful place to spend time with your families or to find some time completely by yourself, if time alone is what you need. My dad always called Lake City, "God's Country," and said when he took a hike in the mountains that it was his church. I'd have to agree with him. The mountains and peaks in our area are magnificent, and there's no doubt in my mind who built them. God gets all the credit. Thousands of people climb Uncompahgre Peak each year – a climb that puts you pretty close to touching heaven. I always wished I could be a tourist in Lake City and just play all summer. But, ever since I was eleven years old, I have worked every summer. It's not easy to make a living here; and I learned at an early age that when work was available, you had to work. So work is what I did, and still do; hopefully retirement is in my future, and I can one day play all summer long.

It was another busy summer; but now, being a grandmother, I felt like I had begun playing a lot more. Watching and trying to see things the way Lane and Shaylee saw things brought a whole new experience for both Robert and me. We were back to playing trucks, throwing balls, hugging stuffed animals, and playing games. Grandchildren are the most wonderful gift God has ever given me, other than my daughter and, of course, Robert and Sweety. Poor Robert, he was always thankful Sweety hadn't been a man. He was pretty sure I would have booted him out the door and Sweety would have moved in and become king of his mansion. If Sweety had been a man, I bet he would have been one handsome guy. I'm sure it would have been like having Matthew McConaughey or Patrick Dempsey around my house. That would just be too much competition for any man. Robert and I laughed about that often. Sweety was so handsome, he could only be compared with men such as that! What a handsome fella!

Back to talking about grandchildren and summer, working and playing. We'd wear ourselves out over those warm days. I would dread the thought of the oncoming winter. The worry of someday not being able to take care of Sweety haunted me. When that day came, my heart would be broken so bad I doubted it would ever heal. The thought of that was a nightmare for me. But, summer was here. Thank God. I enjoyed every second of it and hoped Sweety was getting fat and enjoying the warm days as well.

Where is Sweety?

I wish I didn't have to blink in the summers; they go by so fast. June arrives and before you know it, it's September. Snow can start falling in Lake City in September – not a real welcome sight. I wish there were nine months of summer and three of winter.

It felt like that summer had been extra busy. We were all tired and probably ready for the oncoming slow down, but I knew what winter would mean for me and the stress it would once again bring. Stress or not, I prayed Sweety would show up. Seemed like there were more hunters for the hunting seasons that year. Don was having some problems with trespassers and told me to keep an eye on the lower valley of his ranch for uninvited guests. I would do that for him, as I didn't want hunters sneaking around Sweety's valley. Don was harsh with trespassers and known for it. I was glad he was that way. His harshness protected Sweety.

September went by, and then October went by, and no Sweety. I was a mess; sick with worry. I thought the worst. I'd go and hike up in the mountains and call for him. Several hunters, including Don, told me they were still seeing deer way up high. The early snows hadn't brought them all down. I wasn't sure that was true at the time, and felt I was being told that just to relieve my concern for Sweety. Several of the Riverside bucks had shown up in early October. Squirt was hanging around with Two Cute and a couple more bucks. But, no Beauty and no Sweety, so I had terrible thoughts that I'd lost my two favorites. Every day that Don would walk into the office, I'd ask him if he or any of his hunters had spotted Sweety, or if one of the hunters had killed him. Don would say no and assured me that he had told his hunters about Sweety. I had to trust Don, but I still had that nagging feeling of worry. Trusting an avid hunter and knowing

Sweety was always a hunter's dream buck, the combination was bad. I wanted to trust Don because he had never given me reason not to. But where in the world was my Sweety?

One morning, Don came into where I worked with a big smile on his face and said, "Hey, Karen your buck is coming home." I said, "Are you sure, Don?" After my seeming to doubt him so instantly, he grunted, "Yes I'm sure!" Then Don told me that Sweety was one smart buck. I asked him why. He said he had his rifle sights on him and watched Sweety going through the field with his head and antlers down low as if he was hiding them in the deep, tall grasses. Don said it was pretty amazing to watch and said again, "He's heading to you; he's coming home." Don also said that when Sweety got "home" I should keep him there. "Karen," Don said quietly, "Sweety is huge this year. He is bigger than he's ever been." I wanted so badly to trust Don and be sure he knew who he was seeing. Don seemed adamant though and claimed that, without a doubt, he knew it was Sweety. Again Don warned me of all the hunters who would try and get Sweety if he was spotted. Don wanted to see Sweety survive, so Sweety could breed more Sweetys. Don thought it was good for the whole area to have bucks around such as him. His bloodline was great.

The first thing I did after Don left was call Robert and tell him Don had seen Sweety and thought he was coming home. Robert said, "Are you sure Don knows what Sweety looks like?" I said I felt Don knew it was Sweety because of the thousands of pictures I'd shown him. I prayed Don was right. The seconds, minutes, and hours stood still that day. All I wanted to do after Don had given me the news was go home. Finally three o'clock shined like sunlight on the post office wall. I hurried and finished my books for the day and headed straight home. Even though it was November, I still had a lot of green grass in my yard. We are so protected by all of our trees and our large privacy fence that our yard must have stayed warm. I've noticed our aspen leaves are some of the last to fall around the Lake City area. I walked in the yard and looked around, hoping to see Sweety, but there was no sign of him. The only deer I had in the yard was Squirt, and he was nibbling the last of the green grass still available in the Riverside area. Squirt was so awesome. His antlers were very unique. Squirt was different from all the other bucks. His antlers weren't wide antlers. They went pretty much straight up from the top of his ears, but their thickness and shape were something to see. He was a traffic stopper, and I was sure many hunters wanted to hang his head on their wall.

116

It was a beautiful fall day, and Squirt seemed so relaxed as he grazed in my yard. I sat on the steps of my front porch to watch him for a minute, hoping Sweety would walk in. Then, after a very short time, I heard a snorting, blowing sound coming from the rocks. I knew instantly what the sound was. When a buck threatens another one, he will snort and blow this awful sound. He will hold his head to one side with his ears back and move in the direction of the buck he is threatening. I've watched it many times. Most bucks will move on and try to avoid a confrontation, but some refuse to be pushed.

On this day, though, I'm not sure Squirt realized he was being threatened, because it all happened like lightning had just struck. All hell broke loose. I didn't know for a second or two what was going on. All I knew was Squirt was getting pushed from one end of my yard to the other. It scared me to death, because for a moment I believed Squirt might be killed. I don't think Squirt was even fighting. I'm sure he felt like a Mack truck had just hit him head on and he was trying to figure how the hell he was going to get out of this alive. Although, I'm not sure he had time to think at all.

I knew who the culprit was. The bully who was attacking Squirt for no reason at all was none other than my Sweety. I yelled, "Stop it!" I'm sure Squirt had many different names for Sweety at that moment and "Sweety" was not what Squirt would be calling him just then. Sweety finally stopped pushing Squirt around and looked in my direction and left Squirt standing in a daze. Squirt walked up in the rocks and stood there for at least thirty minutes watching. I was so happy to see Sweety, yet I was a little worried because he trotted right up to me so quickly. He had just been in a vicious fight, and now he was wagging his tail like always and coming straight to me. I had no apples, no cookies, and was afraid just to reach out and hug him. I felt I needed to give him some space after what had just taken place. Don was right, Sweety was huge. He was the biggest I had ever seen him – a monster of a buck. He was nine years old. His body was so muscular, and his antlers were magnificent.

My gentle giant. Looking at him, I was sure he hadn't missed a meal all summer. When Don told me Sweety was bigger, he was talking about Sweety's antler growth. This year Sweety was no longer a five by five. No, this year he was an awesome five by seven; biggest he'd ever been. I understood instantly why Don told me to keep him home. There were so many hunters sneaking around the area. Even though the hunters saw the no hunting signs, they sometimes ignored them. I remembered when we had a buck shot and killed in the upper cemetery. There were houses in every direction, but still the buck was shot there. Protecting Sweety had never been easy; and looking at him now, I knew he'd made my job harder. Oh, but he was so beautiful, and I was so glad to see him.

Sweety was home and bigger than ever. He was a 5 by 7. I was slightly intimidated by his size, but I was glad to see him.

I ran into the house and sliced up several apples and carrots and gave them to Sweety as he stood near the steps of my front porch. He ate from my hands and I petted his wide nose and asked him why he had come home with such a bad attitude toward Squirt? I felt like he was answering me as I looked into his big brown eyes. I said, "You're defending your territory now, huh? You've come home and want it known the king is back and nobody better mess with the king." My yard was Sweety's yard, and he had to keep fear in the other deer. I knew that his being the lead buck wouldn't last forever, and one day I would see another younger, much stronger buck defeat him. Today though, it looked like Sweety had everything under control, and that he wouldn't have too much trouble keeping the other bucks under his hooves.

After he ate the apple, I ran in the house to grab a camera and get some pictures. While I was getting the camera ready, I noticed Sweety climbing up the steps and doing what he had done every year before – eating my potted plants! I went outside, snapped several pictures, and told him that the plants had been waiting there, just for him. I loved watching him as he pulled each stem up and enjoyed what few pansies I had left. I reached out, grabbed our hanging baskets, and set them on the ground. When Sweety was finished with the ones on the porch, he could then devour the baskets that weren't hanging anymore! I couldn't stop smiling at him. I thought of all the years we'd been together. Who would have thought that a wild mule deer buck would befriend someone like me? In my wildest dreams I never thought we'd still be together. There was my baby, larger than life and back in my yard where I prayed he would stay until hunting season was over. We had one more week to go. As smart as Sweety had already proven he was, he should be able to survive the next week. I'd pray for God's help and do whatever I felt I had to do to keep Sweety safe.

Squirt slowly moved out of the yard. He quietly slipped away, hoping he wouldn't draw Sweety's attention. Sweety was so busy eating that he didn't notice Squirt leaving. I felt sorry for Squirt, but I wanted Sweety to always rule my yard. This was his home, his territory. I continued taking pictures of him. He was relaxed and happy. I was relaxed and happy, too.

Squirt

After Sweety had eaten his fill, he went over and laid down under our big pine trees. I hoped he'd stay there all night, but at least he stayed there until Robert got home from work and dusk fell. Both Robert and I were happy he was in our yard where he belonged. We agreed we'd try to keep him in the yard and not try to get him up the hill until hunting season was over. Robert thought his new antlers were beautiful; and he felt, if any hunters spotted him, they would most likely try and tag him.

The next morning Sweety was still hanging out in our yard. He seemed to enjoy grazing and lying around. He liked to lie down near our privacy fence. I think he felt protected there. I went out and gave him a couple of apples for breakfast and petted his beautiful face. I told him to stay in the yard, since there were hunters out there. I think he knew that already, and that was why he'd come home. He was smart. I had to agree with Don. Sweety was smart and, even though the rutting season was beginning, he hopefully would stay in the neighborhood.

As soon as I got to work I wrote a note to Don telling him HE WAS RIGHT! Sweety was HOME! YEAH, YEAH, YEAH! Don came and got his mail, and, when he found the note he walked in the office saying, "I told you so!" He was just a little cocky; he was sure he had been right. Yes, I doubted him! But, I was so glad he was right, I couldn't quit smiling. Don said to keep him in the yard . . . "you still got a week, someone can still shoot him." "Thanks a lot Don," I said, "I was feeling good for a moment, gees!" Don left smiling. I think he enjoyed aggravating me, which he did a good job of and vice versa.

I prayed every time I thought of Sweety. I wanted the week to be over, and then I would worry about the winter. Beauty still hadn't shown up, so I felt I probably was right and that he had been the buck hit by the car. I hated that. Sly, now Beauty, who would be next? Orphan had come in two weeks earlier than Sweety. I hoped she had a fawn, as the year before I had witnessed Beauty breeding her; but there was no fawn with Orphan. She had not had a fawn yet, and I wondered if she ever would. Maybe her small size prevented her from having babies. I really wanted her to have a fawn, because I would then have felt we had a little Beauty still running around. Orphan and Sweety were still close, and she would follow him around and lie next to him if he lay down. Watching them together made me happy; but knowing that Sweety was already nine years old, I wondered how much longer we would be together.

I had often heard that deer didn't live much more than ten years. I knew that a buck we called Star and also Bruiser both had lived to at least fourteen. That was my guess, as they seemed to be have been around the area forever, and I had met them when they were already full grown. They both had long lives. Hopefully Sweety would have a long life like the two of them. When Star got old, however, he got real crippled. I wouldn't want that for Sweety. Poor Bruiser lost most of his teeth, which caused his death. I wish all the deer could live to old age, but there were so many things that could cut their lives short. If it wasn't a predator after them, then there was the danger of getting hit by a car, shot by a hunter, or getting caught in barb wire fences.

Chapter 36

Care Giving

Another hunting season was over and done! Sweety was still with me, along with Squirt, Two Cute, and many more. Two Cute had grown to be pretty awesome himself. They all were awesome. I was so relieved to get through hunting season and have them all survive. Now I had to train them once again to go up to the little valley if they wanted any treats. Training them was easier this time. Sweety would follow right behind me or walk with me. I loved having him by my side. Two Cute would walk close to me at times, yet for some reason I didn't trust him nearly as much as I trusted some of the others. He had a certain look in his eyes that made me wonder. I just had a feeling inside of me that I needed to be careful around him. He was getting so large, and he was tough. I felt if Sweety lost his status in the herd, it would be because Two Cute had taken over. Sweety didn't like him all that much either, but he let him tag along with him anyway. Robert thought Two Cute was really something because his antlers had gotten so thick and had so many knots by the base of the horns. He was pretty, but I felt he was a threat to Sweety and perhaps to me, so I often chased him away when he came too close.

The rutting season brought several new bucks into the area. Sweety was so large that I didn't see too many attempt to fight him, so he got to do a lot of romancing that winter. I believed the next summer we would have lots of little, sweet Sweety's running around. That was a great thought, and something to look forward to.

When winter set in, it set in pretty hard – cold and snowy. Robert would have to go to work by seven most mornings, so we were always getting up early. We would drink our coffee and visit with each other before he headed off to work. One morning I was cleaning and straightening up the house, when I saw Sweety coming into my backyard, leaping and jumping and acting crazy. I could see something was wrong with his right back leg. I put my coat and boots on and ran outside to see what was wrong with him. Sweety was panicking. I saw a piece of wood stuck in his back hoof. It had to be very painful by the way he

was acting. I tried to calm him, but he must have been hurting very bad, and I couldn't get him to calm down. I knew I had to do something fast or he was going to injure himself worse than he already was. I kept talking to him and following him as he leaped and kicked around the yard. I could tell he was tired, and I worried he had really hurt his hoof.

This piece of wood was embedded in Sweety's hoof.

The piece of wood had a cross-looking effect to it and was imbedded in the split of his hoof. I kept trying to get close to him, but I would back off when it seemed he was going to jump or leap high in the air again. Finally he let me touch his neck, and I talked to him calmly. He seemed a little less nervous. I knew I had to take my chances and move quickly. I pushed Sweety's head away from me and jumped on the small piece of wood with my feet. My weight and Sweety jumping in the air at the same time pulled the stick from his hoof. I had the wood in my hand, and Sweety had a big look of relief all over his beautiful face. I was thankful he didn't hurt me, as crazy as he was acting. Instantly he was the same sweet animal he had always been. I checked him out to see that he was walking okay, and he was. He was lucky, and I was lucky. I thanked God and Daddy and everyone up in heaven for helping me. I believed they were all giving me a helping hand. What would Sweety and I go through next? My heart was beating pretty fast, and both my knees were shaking. I kissed Sweety on his nose, and he licked my face with his huge tongue. Sweety was okay, and that was all I wanted. I had helped him, and it felt great. One more thing that we would go through that would make me love him even more.

Chapter 37

Thank You, Don

I was busier this winter than usual, as my co-worker took a three-week vacation and Beth, my boss, had several things she had to get done. Robert and I were planning a trip in May to South Dakota with a swing through Wyoming, so I needed the hours. I couldn't spend much time with Sweety, at least not as much as I would have liked. But, every evening I would try and be with him for at least thirty or so minutes. He loved attention, just like all my pets did. He acted sad some days when I would have to hurry off. He'd hang his big head and sometimes act like a child would and pout. I'd turn around and go back to give him an extra carrot or apple and one more kiss on the nose. I hated leaving him. I enjoyed his company and felt more comfortable among the deer than in a crowd of people.

The morning of January 24th, Sweety walked in the yard without his seven point antler. Robert and I went outside and looked frantically for it. We both wanted that antler more than any of his others, as it was his biggest. We found nothing and had to go to work. That afternoon we could search for it again. We searched and combed the Riverside area the best we could without intruding into our neighbors' yards. I was very selfish when it came to Sweety and sharing his magnificent antlers with someone else. Even Robert couldn't claim them if he had found them. I was pretty determined to find that special antler. Every free moment I had, I went looking. A couple of mornings later Sweety dropped the other antler, which I quickly found. I was thankful I had at least that one, but I still badly wanted the other one. After a month of hunting without finding the antler I began to give up. I thought that Sweety probably dropped it in someone's yard and they had my treasure. I hated that thought. I had every antler of Sweety's except for one that I couldn't find several years ago. Now I couldn't find his biggest. Robert got tired of combing the area and searching for something he felt we didn't have a chance of finding. I finally agreed with him.

February came and went, and March came and went, and still no antler. We had a lot of antler hunters out and about. It was fun to hunt for them, and several local people loved to do it as much as I did. One evening I took a walk up the mountain and Sweety tagged along with me. I kept asking him, "Where did you lose that antler?" I sure wished he could talk. It was a quiet night, and the moon was shining so bright. It wasn't all that cold. I came back and sat on my porch for awhile, just enjoying the night. I could have sworn I saw the headlights of a vehicle high up near the cliff area on the ranch that Don took care of. I thought, "Why is someone up there at this time of night." It seemed awful late for anyone to be up there. I watched for awhile. The light finally disappeared or was shut off. Seeing the light bothered me all night. I wondered if someone was trespassing on Don's land. I thought that maybe they might be trying to poach an animal. It was odd. I didn't feel that it was the moonlight, but it might have been. I lay awake and thought of a thousand things that someone might be doing up there that late at night. None of my thoughts were good. I always think the worst – a very bad habit of mine. It was a long night, and it was all my fault that I lost sleep.

The next morning was on a Saturday, and I always had to work on Saturdays. I hoped Don would come in so I could ask him if he had been on the upper ranch the evening before. Don walked in around eleven that morning, and as he was getting his mail I walked over to his post office box and asked him to come into the office. When Don came in, I told him about the headlights I thought I had seen and asked if he had someone up there that late at night? Don said no, there shouldn't have been anyone up there. He said it was probably the moonlight. I always argued with Don! I told him, no, I really thought someone was up there. Don knew I hadn't found Sweety's antler, and he knew how crazy I was about Sweety. I'm sure he thought, "This woman is losing her mind," but he must have listened to me anyway.

Sunday morning Robert and I got up, packed a lunch, and thought we would take a hike up to Station Eleven. We tried to hike up there every spring. It was a popular hike for many, and the scenery was beautiful. As Robert and I neared the small peak, I began glassing the area. We were on the side opposite the upper ranch, so I looked through my binoculars in the ranch's direction. I always wondered if I could spot Sweety and his gang. I did spot something; not Sweety, but someone on a 4-wheeler driving around the area. I told Robert to look through his binoculars to see if he could see the man or woman on the 4-wheeler. Robert spotted him, and we both felt it was Don checking the ranch. I told Robert that I'd mentioned to Don what I thought I saw on the upper ranch, and he must have gone to check to see if everything was all right. I looked a couple of times, watching Don as he drove around the ranch. I saw him park the 4-wheeler and get off and take a walk up the meadow. I thought to myself, and laughed out loud, "Boy, Don would be pissed if he knew I was spying on him." For some reason though I was very curious about what Don was doing. I watched him walk back, get on the 4-wheeler, then drive away. I couldn't find him anymore, so we continued our hike.

The next morning at work, I noticed Don's pickup truck pull up beside the office in front of the window where my stamp drawer was. I watched Don get out of his truck with this big grin on his face. I opened my window, and he motioned for me to come out. I told Beth that Don wanted me to see something, and she said for me to go. I ran out the back door, and as I came around the corner I saw Don opening his door and pulling out this huge antler. I knew whose antler it was. It was Sweety's. Don just handed it to me. He said he had talked with his wife Sue and they both agreed to give it to me. I cried. I laughed. I threw my arms around Don! I could not thank him enough. I told him thank God I got him worried about someone maybe being up on the ranch, and he agreed he wouldn't have gone up there if I hadn't said what I did. I kissed the antler, hugged it, and thanked Don a thousand times. I knew how beautiful this antler was, and most guys wouldn't have given it to me. I told Don I would treasure it. What a gift and what a special man Don was for giving it to me. I also thanked Sue for letting him give it to me! I was blessed with good friends. I told Don that Robert and I had watched him with our binoculars from Station Eleven, and I was wondering like crazy what he was doing. He shook his head and said, Karen you are crazy! Crazy or not, I now finally had Sweety's largest antler. I was so glad Don had gone up on the ranch. Again and again I thanked him.

I went in the office and showed Beth Sweety's antler. She knew how badly I wanted to find it. Robert had driven up while Don was giving me the antler, so he already knew my good news. I was so excited. God Bless Don Cardin!

Most women love diamonds and pearls. I loved Sweety's antlers and music. If I could have those two luxuries in my life, I was pretty happy. I was thrilled to finally have Sweety's antler, and the way it all happened was great. Don was supposed to go to the upper ranch that day; there were no "ifs," "ands," or "buts" about it! Funny how things happen, I believe it was meant to be. I was meant to get Sweety's antler, and I'm so glad it was Don Cardin who found it, because otherwise I doubt it would be mine today.

Sweety's lifetime of antler growth. I feel so blessed to have found all but one antler.
Sweety's antlers are my diamonds.

Chapter 38
Bad News

We took Lane and Shaylee fishing as often as we could. It was so much fun just watching them get so excited when a fish took their bait. We would help them reel the fish in. Both Lane and Shaylee's eyes would get big, and they would jump up and down with excitement. We spent a lot of weekends fishing with them and having family picnics. Jennifer and Justin hardly got to keep their babies on the weekends. Lane and Shaylee were such a giant blessing in our lives. No more dull times! They kept everyone on the move, and we saw things through their young eyes, which put a bright and new perspective on everything!

Summer was coming to an end and September was near. I hadn't gotten to visit much with Don or Sue that summer. They were busy, just like everyone was. Don seemed a little more stressed than in past years. He was traveling somewhere nearly every week, and if you got a chance to see him it was, "Hi, bye, have a good day," and that was about it. I didn't think much about it, because if you wanted to make money you had to work extra hard in the summers. Well, it was the first week in September when Don walked into the office and said he needed to talk to both Beth and me. Don said he wanted to let us know, before anyone else told us, that he and Sue were planning on moving to Texas in December. I hated hearing that news. I had to leave the room for a moment because the tears were coming and I couldn't fight them. I didn't say anything much because I couldn't talk; Don hurried and left. I should have known he was planning to move, because he had a young man he had been training for some time to help with the ranch. All I could think of was what a loss it was going to be for Lake City.

Don's wife Sue was like a bright shining star. She could walk in our office and light up the whole place. Sue worked at our local bank, and any time you walked in there she greeted you with a smile. She was so pleasant and just a fun loving person to be around. No doubt, she would be missed. Don was such a buddy, and his involvement with the wildlife was huge. He fought for a lot of things to improve our deer and elk herds and made things happen. I always thought either he or Sue would make terrific county commissioners. I loved the way they viewed things, and they weren't afraid to speak out about things that needed to be spoken out about. Don was about the only one I told my deep dark secrets about Sweety to, other than my family. He watched over my Sweety. I was hurting over their moving and dreading December when I would have to tell them goodbye.

This was not going to be my winter. Don and Sue were leaving; but then I got the news that my two friends who had let me take care of Sweety on their land were also selling and moving. I wasn't prepared for all this and was really having a tough time accepting it. I had to accept it, though, and make the best of it. Don did come in and ask me if I would consider helping the young man out at times at the ranch, if he needed the help. I was more than glad to help, since Don had done so much for me. I believe that Don was asking me to do this because it would let me watch for Sweety myself, since he couldn't be there. I could go and search for Sweety and not be trespassing. I was thankful for that, and I loved the ranch and would protect what was there and what lived on it.

Chapter 39

Sweety's Territory

I didn't have to ask Don to look for Sweety this fall, and I didn't have to worry or search for him either. September 10th, Sweety, along with Two Cute and Trouble, walked into the yard. Sweety came down early; what a huge surprise! Seeing him was the best thing that had happened in the recent weeks. He had declined though. Sweety was no longer a five by seven. He was still a five by five, but much smaller. His antlers weren't as thick and the tines weren't as long. He still was a huge buck, but I could see he was showing his age.

Sweety and I greeted each other as we had always done. Two long lost friends. It was a happy event. He climbed up on the deck and helped himself to my still colorful pansies. I told him that I wished he wouldn't eat them yet, as they were still blooming and it hadn't gotten cold enough to kill them. He ignored everything I said. After my pansies were all in his stomach, he looked at me like, "Go get an apple for me, Karen!" I was not prepared for him to come down so soon and was completely out of apples. I had some peanut butter cookies – the marmots' cookies – and that was the best I could do for him until I could get to the store. He liked the cookies and seemed satisfied. I told him that I would go buy apples, and I said "I love you so much and it's so good to see you." He wagged his tail. I loved that. It was a happy sign that he loved me back. He went over by our big privacy fence and lay down. Trouble and Two Cute followed him, and both stretched out beside Sweety. I ran in, got my camera, and took pictures of the three of them. Trouble still had velvet falling from his antlers, and Two Cute had a little bit of velvet left. I noticed how big Two Cute had gotten. I knew Sweety was getting older and Two Cute was getting tougher and bigger. Sweety seemed to still have their respect, and I prayed he could keep it. Rutting season was still far away and hopefully, for now at least, the three would remain at peace with each other.

Robert and Shaylee shared birthdays, and we made that a special day. The entire family got together for a barbeque over at Jennifer's and Justin's. Robert and I both would buy Lane a present on Shaylee's birthday, and we would buy Shaylee a present on Lane's birthday. It was fun to watch them enjoy each other's birthday. Robert didn't get as many presents as the kids. He kind of got short-changed now since he had to share his day with a sweet little girl. Robert didn't mind!

Don and Sue were planning for their move in December. I told Don about Sweety coming in, and I think he was glad. He was probably happy that I wouldn't be putting any pressure on him to look for Sweety. He knew I still wanted him to tell his hunters not to shoot my Sweety, so the pressure wasn't entirely off. Sweety didn't seem to want to run off. He hung around my yard and ate the green grass and just relaxed. He seemed content to be where he was, and I was more than happy to have him where I knew he was safe. I loved coming home and having him greet me. I did buy apples; but natural food was plentiful, and I wasn't concerned that he wasn't getting enough to eat. He looked round and healthy. The only thing that worried me was that he had some stiffness in his shoulder, which I had seen before. I think he had arthritis in it. You could see that there were days it would really bother him, and then days he didn't seem to have any trouble at all.

The fall colors were magnificent that year, and people came from all over to enjoy the beauty. I enjoyed this time of year and usually looked forward to it. I was having a hard time though. I knew hunting season was coming, and I knew winter was coming. Both hunting season and

Top - Trouble
Middle - Two Cute
Bottom - Sweety
They all loved the safety of my yard.

winter had become bad words to me. By now Sweety and I had been through a lot of hunting seasons and winters together. We both were tired of them. Just the thought of being hunted every year must be awful. Just the thought of having a severe winter and fighting to survive is awful. I was afraid that Sweety wouldn't make it without me. I'd lost his feeding grounds, and I knew he had never survived a winter without some help. I know deer survived without me before, but Sweety had never been without my help. Could he survive without it now? I didn't have an answer and would put it all in God's hands.

Hunting season came, and there were more hunters driving around the Riverside area than I had ever seen before. Sweety refused to go far from the yard. He liked a corner of my yard and was not interested in going much further. I didn't want hunters driving by and stopping, so I would go outside and threaten them with evil looks. I didn't say anything, but they got the message by my frowning at them. I seemed to be frowning so much it felt like I was losing my smile. Clouds were rolling in; snow wasn't far away. I knew I'd be saying goodbye to some special friends and didn't have an answer from God yet on how to take care of Sweety. I was blue and sad. There were many things to think and worry about.

Deer were coming down as October ended and November waltzed in. We had a buck come into our yard that I had never seen before. He was the grumpiest looking animal, so I named him ''Grumpy.'' Sweety was not happy to see this new buck in his yard, and a fight broke out instantly. Sweety quickly made Grumpy aware of who was king of the yard. Grumpy had no status at all. There was no doubt about it. Grumpy seemed to get Sweety's message. I worried they would fight again as the rutting season neared, but for now Sweety had taken charge. Grumpy seemed to want to stay among the Riverside herd even though he was not welcomed. Two Cute and everyone else also tried pushing him out, but Grumpy did not want to leave. He would stand his ground with the rest of the group, though he would move away as Sweety approached him. I could tell his attitude could be a problem, and I hated seeing him trying to stay in the area. I had a feeling that if Two Cute didn't become king and take Sweety's place, then Grumpy would be among the herd in time. I knew from seeing Sweety's decline that it was just a matter of time. He would not rule my yard much longer. Instead, he would be ruled.

Two Cute was giving it all he had to rule Sweety. Sweety would move from one end of our yard to the other to avoid Two Cute if he came near. It was apparent that Two Cute knew Sweety was getting older, and he had the advantage over him. Yet I never saw them fight. They must have had a mutual respect for one another, since they grew up in the same herd.

A day or two after the last deer season was over, Robert and I heard gun shots one evening. The shots sounded like they came from below us, at a place we called Pete's Lake. We thought it was odd to hear shots that late at night, and we both wondered who was shooting. Pete's Lake is just on the northern outskirts of town. Through the years it seemed that if we lost a Riverside buck it would be after the season closed. Someone would sneak around and poach a deer. It must have come from the desperation of not getting an animal, and the hunter was in need of the meat. The next morning I made sure Sweety was alright, but I noticed Two Cute was nowhere to be seen. I asked the sheriff if they had a report of a shooting the night before and they had not. I told him what we had heard and was just curious why someone would be shooting that late at night. I had no proof and there was nothing I could do, but I believed someone had attempted to poach a deer that night.

I couldn't tell anyone that Two Cute was missing. I wanted to call out search and rescue to find him. He was a Riverside buck, and he was missing. Someone surely should have had me committed back in those days. I hated Two Cute being gone. He was so beautiful. After a couple of days without him coming in the yard or seeing him around the area, I felt sure he had been killed. I thought about it a lot, and my answer to myself was God probably saw him as a threat to Sweety and knew that something had to be done. Sweety didn't seem to mind Two Cute's disappearance. Robert didn't like it though. He thought Two Cute was a great buck and hoped he would breed the does in the area because his bloodline was so good.

The holiday season had begun. Every Thanksgiving we would meet with my daughter's husband's family and go out to dinner in Almont, Colorado, at a neat little restaurant located there. We always took a friend, Terry Hall, with us. He was an older gentleman we had befriended many years before, who had become a huge part of our family. It was always a nice dinner, and we would have a great time together. We would take a lot of photographs of everyone, as Justin's grandmother was getting very old. Shaylee was fun to watch at that age, and she seemed to like older folks. She would cuddle right up to them and talk and talk. Justin's grandmother was so impressed with little Shaylee. We all thought to ourselves that one day Shaylee might become a nurse because of her concern for older people. Family gatherings were always great and much more special with the little ones and the older ones being there. I looked forward to holidays just to get with everyone. They were special times.

Chapter 40

A Sad December

I've always looked forward to the holidays, but I sure wasn't looking forward to the next ten days. Don and Sue were leaving the first week of December. I dreaded saying goodbye. What a loss for Lake City; I must have told myself that a thousand times. I could and would willingly pack up some people and help them move, but not Don and Sue. I wanted to put nails in their tires, and kick and scream like a baby throwing a tantrum. I didn't want them to leave. It wasn't like we ever got to really visit or go out as two couples. It was my being so comfortable around them. I didn't feel judged, and we had a lot in common. I couldn't say that about almost anyone else. I have always been pretty much a loner, so I treasured the friendship I had found in them. Then there was the Sweety thing too! If Don wasn't there to watch what the hunters did, my Sweety would be in more danger. I was hurting. Don would walk in nearly every day and usually say something just to irritate me. I was half angry at the two of them for even considering moving, so I usually said something half mean back to him. This wasn't all that uncommon, as we had done this sort of thing for years. It took a long time to like Don in the beginning. He was pretty hard on the Post Office. He must have had some bad experiences. You liked Sue the instant you met her. Don took awhile! Being cocky, that was his problem, but after a time I learned to like and respect him more than I ever dreamed possible. It just took work.

Don and Sue Cardin with their dog Jaz.

The third of December came way too fast. I slowly got myself dressed that morning and

133

fought back tears, while I brushed my teeth and tried to fix my face. I shouldn't have even attempted putting make-up on. I was just going to mess that job up completely! I'd be telling the Cardins goodbye in just a few hours. I felt like I was going to a funeral.

Sue bounced in first. You could recognize Sue's voice a mile away, and I listened as she told several people goodbye while walking into the office. So many of the townspeople hated seeing her leave! I choked up pretty quick and told her I hated them leaving. Lake City wouldn't be the same. We hugged each other, cried, and out the door she went saying Don would be by soon. Well, it was about thirty minutes later when I saw Don pull up by my window. Darn how I hated telling him goodbye. He had sure been a good buddy. I'm sure I looked like someone had beaten me with a bat. I just couldn't quit crying, and my eyes had swollen pretty good. I was so sick and tired of all the changes that were happening and that I could do nothing about it. Don said he'd be back, and for me to help out at the ranch if I was needed, and to keep an eye on Sweety. I hugged him and told him goodbye, and he left pretty quickly. I cried the rest of the day and probably on and off for the next couple of days. I'd miss them a lot and knew it was going to be tough without them around. Life goes on; change happens. I didn't like it.

Don Cardin on one of his many hunting adventures.

What could possibly happen next? It must have been about three nights after Don and Sue left Lake City when Robert and I heard a pretty bad deer fight going on in the back of our yard. We went out and shined our flashlights on the two deer that were battling. I knew one of the bucks was my Sweety, but it took a minute or two before I recognized the other. We had named the other buck "Slick," as his coat was so smooth and slick. He sometimes looked like a statue, almost perfect in his looks. They had taken their fight clear up on the mountain side, and all you could hear were antlers clashing together. Again, there was nothing I could do but pray they both would be alright. Rutting season had begun, and fighting was common this time of year. Fighting over women, how goofy! Sweety was fighting for his leadership and women, and the younger bucks were fighting to take over his kingdom. I didn't sleep that night for fear Sweety had been hurt in the battle. I hadn't even begun taking care of Sweety that winter. An apple or two was about all I could do, and now he was in trouble and I could do nothing. I just had the hardest time accepting the way things were. I felt lost at times.

The next morning I stared out my window, praying to see Sweety and worrying. Sweety finally walked into the yard, but he wasn't walking right. I ran out to him and could see he had a bloody gash in his right front leg. It was bad. It was real bad. I knew I would have to doctor it, and I knew I had to start right then. I went back into the house and fixed some apples, carrots, and grain and took all of it out to him. I went back into the house and gathered wet rags, peroxide, and Neosporin. I went to Sweety and gently talked to him, asking for his leg. He was hurting, and he was cranky. I knew he could hurt me, yet I had to doctor his leg. I bent down to the bloody gash. Sweety watched my every move. I kept talking to him, telling him I had to put medicine on his leg and he had to let me do it. I would grab a slice of apple and kiss his nose and tell him it's okay. He didn't seem to mind my wiping the blood away. When I poured peroxide on it, though, he did jump a little and went backwards. I was glad he went backwards. I was totally putting myself in harm's way of his antlers. If he'd wanted, he could have done some damage. I grabbed another apple and repeated pouring peroxide on his wound. He seemed to acknowledge what I was trying to do and calmed down. After I cleaned his wound with peroxide, I rubbed it with a complete tube of Neosporin. I knew that I would have to repeat this every chance I got until I saw him heal.

Day and night I did this faithfully. I bought ten tubes of Neosporin and several bottles of peroxide. Sweety had a couple of days when his leg was badly swollen. I would check his eyes and nose to make sure they looked alright. If I saw any mucus coming from his eyes, I would know that he had an infection. I knew what I had to look for. I'd seen other deer throughout the years die from their injuries. I was so worried, trying to care for him, and praying no one would see me. God forbid if they did. If someone tried to stop me, it would absolutely kill me. He needed my attention now more than ever.

Talk about depressed! Life sucked at that moment. According to the law I was wrong for trying to save something. At the very least, I would not get any support. I would have given the world for them just to let me heal Sweety. I felt I wasn't doing him harm in my heart; I hadn't stolen the wild out of him. He roamed free and wild every summer until the snows came – all of the deer did. Sweety needed a veterinarian to look at his leg, and had he been a horse I could have gotten him that help. It all made me so sick; it seemed so unfair. My stomach burned like fire. I felt so sorry for Sweety, and pretty sorry for myself.

I was bitter! I hated myself for being like this. I wanted the Division of Wildlife to help me save Sweety, but instead I feared them. I shouldn't have been so hard on them since I had never asked for help. Maybe they would help Sweety, but what if they wouldn't? I had heard where a cow elk had befriended a woman in the Rocky Mountain National Forest and they were discovered by a woman wildlife officer. That wildlife officer had the elk put down. I couldn't take that chance. I would just do everything I could to make him well.

Sweety came to visit for Christmas.

Sweety knew what I was trying to do for him. There was no doubt when he began lifting his leg for me to pour and rub the medicine on the gash. I loved this animal so much. Dear God how I loved him. The two of us were quite a pair. He was a mess and I was a basket case. Together though, we were going to do all we could to get him better and ease my mind.

Finally the swelling began to come down! I thanked God a million times. Sweety still had a slight limp, but he was getting better. Christmas was here; Sweety seemed fine. That was the best Christmas gift I could get. I had friends over, and Sweety came to visit. They enjoyed him so much, just by watching him and me together. Lane and Shaylee had gone to their other grandparents' house for Christmas, so I spent that day with friends, Robert, and Sweety. Steve and Vickie Bales were old friends of mine. Steve had dated my sister Cindy.

In fact he was dating her at the time of her death. Steve and I remained close friends and had even dated each other for awhile. I was like his little sister though, and being friends was our best solution for the relationship. He loved hunting and, like my real brother Steve, once said, he also would like to hunt in my yard. Steve Bales always threatened that. Steve and Vicky both took several pictures of Sweety that day. Sweety was such an attention grabber! He stuck his big head through an opened window in our dining room. He stayed with us all Christmas Day.

I fixed Sweety special treats for Christmas and ran off all the other deer, so he would know he was special. I didn't want the other deer around him at that time because I was trying to get him completely healed. Orphan was the only one I let hang around. I knew she was no threat. Sweety made that Christmas special for me because he was getting well, and I knew he was because of me. It was so apparent to everyone how much Sweety and I both loved each other. Steve and Vicky both couldn't believe the kind of relationship we had. They said he acted as if he were our dog. He was our dog, just slightly larger than most dogs!

I didn't know that this would be the last picture taken of Sweety.

My beautiful Sweety.

Chapter 41

Poor Grumpy

Usually around Christmas time the rutting season was drawing to an end. I was glad. This meant the fighting between the bucks was almost over. Sweety didn't need to get into anymore confrontations. I wanted him to quit limping and get back to his healthy, normal self. Every day he seemed better. The wound had scabbed over and the swelling was gone. A small bump about three inches long was all I could see on his front leg, just below the knee and right above his hoof. I had spoiled him during those three weeks, and he took full advantage of my attention. But, winter came on pretty strong right after Christmas, and I knew I had to try to find a spot for Sweety and some of his buddies if I were to help them out. Sweety had been in my yard since September. I'd made no effort to move him, as hardly any of the other deer were hanging around and also because of his injury. I figured all I could do was try and get them behind a very large rock that was up the mountain. It was hidden from the road, and maybe I could spend time with them there. That was the only plan I could come up

with. I decided to wait though, until I knew Sweety was completely healed and had no more limp. I told myself that if I got a ticket I got a ticket. Sweety was more important than money to me. I'd have done jail time for him.

The morning of the 29th of December, Robert received a phone call from his brother Ronnie. Ronnie lived in Idaho, and they didn't get to see each other much. When Robert receives a phone call from family, you can count on them talking a long time. I'd had my morning coffee and decided I'd walk out and see if Sweety was in the yard. I fixed him some breakfast too, a combination of everything I knew he loved, and went out to call him. It was only a second or two before Sweety came around the corner of one of the sheds, still limping slightly. I said, "Good morning, Sweetheart. How are you today?" He wagged his tail and trotted over for his goodies. As I fed him and talked with him, I could hear noise from the back of our yard and Sweety kept looking in that direction. I knew something had to be wrong, because I could hear groaning and flopping and hitting sounds, but I couldn't see anything until Sweety and I started to walk toward the noise. All of a sudden I saw a large buck tossing his entire body back and forth over a large rock and around a tall pine tree. I knew the buck was tangled in something, and by the way he was throwing his body around, I knew he was badly tangled.

I ran into the house and yelled at Robert that a buck was tangled up in a rope or something up in the rocks. I grabbed a sharp knife and took off. When I got outside, I heard even more banging and groaning than before. I couldn't believe what was happening. Sweety had gone up to where the buck was and was trying to kill him. I'm not sure why Sweety was doing such a thing, except maybe he felt he would put the animal out of his misery. I yelled and yelled at Sweety to stop, but he continued. As I approached the tangled buck, I saw it was Grumpy – the meanest buck we had in the area, and the one buck Sweety had no use for. I still had to try and save him. Sweety was pushing him up against our metal building and putting dents in it. Grumpy would try and dart away, but he was wrapped so tightly with rope around his antlers and a tree that he could only run about eight or ten feet in any direction. Each time he tried to get away, he threw his body over a large rock, and it looked like he was going to break his neck. I screamed for Robert's help, but I knew I had no time to waste. I had to do something fast. Grumpy would die if I didn't.

I couldn't get between Grumpy and Sweety because I would be killed. I repeatedly yelled and screamed at Sweety to stop. I yelled "GET BACK SWEETY, STOP IT!" I yelled, I cried, and I could tell every time I yelled it bothered Sweety. I began crying as I screamed, and all of a sudden Sweety stopped. He looked at me, turned away from the exhausted Grumpy, and limped away. I hated yelling at Sweety like that, but I had no choice. I'd never yelled at Sweety, and my heart was breaking. He hung his head as he moved away. Grumpy was afraid of me and was in a complete state of panic. I had to yell at him to stay back, so I could get close to the rope that was wrapped at least twenty times around the trunk of the tree. Both of Grumpy's antlers were tangled in the rope.

When I tried to get close to the tree, Grumpy would leap right at me and throw his entire body in my direction, jerking his head completely backwards. I knew at any minute he would snap his neck. He had come down so hard against the rock, so many times, that he had to be injuring himself. I had to free him quickly. I continued trying to cut the rope during the time between his leaps and my own attempts to avoid him hitting me. He was completely worn out and, finally after one more of my screams, he stopped his leaping and gave me enough time to cut through the inch thick rope that had entangled him. Grumpy was free and alive. I was exhausted and trembling. Grumpy stared at me with his dark eyes for several minutes. He moved his neck around. When he realized he could freely move, he looked at me again and slowly walked in my direction, stopping several times as if he had something to say to me. I said, "I saved you Grumpy." I cried and he watched me. He walked around the rock and then turned back and stood and looked one more time at me. I believe in his way he was thanking me. There was something about the way his dark brown eyes looked at me with a softness I'd never seen from him.

Grumpy walked off into the trees and went to the lower valley; and I went to Sweety, begging for his forgiveness. He was confused about my screaming at him and I knew it. I could see he really wanted to be alone, and he turned away from me. I was sick about what had just happened, and yet so thankful Grumpy was alive. I talked to Sweety for several minutes, telling him I loved him and I just didn't want him killing Grumpy. He finally let me kiss his nose and rub his head. We were okay. I could not damage this special friendship, and I continued loving on him until I knew everything was right between us. Sweety followed me back to the yard, and I went in the house half angry at Robert for not helping me. He was still on the phone talking to his brother, but my yelling at him made him hang the phone up. He instantly told me to shut up! He yelled those damn deer were a damn nightmare to him. I yelled back, and this went on for several minutes. Too many emotions came out all at once, and I hurled them all at Robert. He hurled them right back, and we both went in opposite directions, wishing our house was much larger so we could be as far away as possible from one another. Finally we both apologized and everything calmed back down. Robert and Sweety were no longer mad at me, I was no longer mad at Robert for not helping me, and Grumpy had been saved. So all in all, everything seemed okay again.

Chapter 42

My World Falls Apart

January 2005 arrived with a snowstorm. Several inches of the white stuff blanketed the mountains. I had prayed that 2005 would be a better year than 2004. I had no idea what heartache was going to hit me next. I was busy at work. Right after Christmas there seemed to be a ton of junk mail arriving, so I was putting in a lot of hours at the office. Sweety still had a slight limp, so I wasn't trying to get him up the mountain yet. Grumpy was hanging around the yard, and so was Squirt. I knew that soon I'd have to make the effort of getting them to leave. I fed Sweety his usual apples and shared some of them with both Grumpy, Squirt, and of course little Orphan. I could hand-feed everyone but Grumpy; but I thought that after all he and I had been through, I would try and see if he would eat from my hand. My first attempt to hand-feed him succeeded with little effort. He ate out of my hand, watching me with that sincere look he had had the day I rescued him. I guess I'd made a friend. I smiled at him. What a grumpy old man he had been, but now he seemed so much different. I didn't try to give him much attention, as I knew my Sweety didn't care for him and I didn't want him to hang around our yard all that often. Sweety was the most important deer to me. He came first in everything that involved deer!

Well, I sure wasn't prepared for what was about to happen next. It was the morning of January 4th. It was very cold and Sweety walked up to my kitchen window with frost on his face. I could see nothing wrong with him, so I cut up some apples and carrots and went out to give him his breakfast. I handed him an apple and he dropped it. I handed him another and he dropped it. I tried a carrot and it also fell to the ground. He snorted in aggravation and I knew something was wrong. I sat the bowl of apples down and picked his head up to look into his mouth. Tears began flooding down my face as I looked at his front teeth. They had been completely pushed forward, and one was gone. The others hung loosely. Oh Dear God, Sweety, what did you do? What happened to you my sweet Sweety? I knew by just looking at him that he would never pull another strand of grass from the ground again. Oh my God, he was going to die and I knew it. I grabbed his head, held him, and burst into tears. What could I do? If only Phil Mason was still alive, he would help me. I needed a dentist! I needed one now!

I had to go to work. I didn't want to leave Sweety, but I had no answers. I called Robert, crying so hard he couldn't understand one word I was saying. He came right up to the yard and looked at Sweety and said, "Honey there's nothing you can do. You'll have to hand feed him from now on." I picked up the apples and tried poking them back far enough to where he could chew and swallow them. He ate some, but he didn't eat much. Sweety was agitated that he couldn't pick up the apples himself, and I felt like I was dying inside. He tried to walk away, but I made him come back because I didn't want him to leave. He followed me back and once again I got him to eat a little more, but he didn't stay long. I cried as I watched him leave my yard. I kept trying to get him to stay, but I couldn't. I was insane with worry. I prayed to God. I prayed to Daddy. I begged and pleaded for help. Please, please help me to help Sweety, please . . . .

I wanted to stay home that day, find Sweety, and stay with him. I wanted to call Beth and tell her I couldn't come to work. I picked up the phone ten times, but then set it back down. My staying with Sweety wouldn't fix what was wrong. I couldn't quit praying. I needed a miracle to fix what was wrong with Sweety. I even bargained with God, telling him I'd never do anything slightly wrong again and tried to work out a deal with him. I was desperate and so scared for Sweety. During his whole life I made sure he was fed, and now he would starve to death right in front of me. He loved his apples and carrots. He loved his grain. He loved eating every flower in my yard. My heart was breaking into a million pieces, and I couldn't stop crying. I went on to work anyway but couldn't talk at all or I would cry. Beth and Trish both knew something was wrong, but I told them I couldn't talk at that time about it. The hours dragged, even though we were busy. I looked at the clock every chance I got, and it didn't seem to budge. I wanted to go home.

Finally I was on my way. The minute I got there, I went inside and cut apples and carrots and crackers into small bites and went in search for Sweety. I

My gentle friend, how I miss you!

searched and searched until dark. Finally I went home and tried to cook supper for Robert. Robert kept saying, "He will come in; he always does. Calm down Karen." I was miles away from being calm. I felt like I was losing my mind with worry. Jennifer called and we talked for a long time. She would say, "Mom you've done everything you can do for Sweety." She was crying too. She knew how much I loved him, and Sweety was loved by the entire family. Sweety was loved! There was no doubt about it. Where was he? Why hadn't he come down yet? Why wasn't he lying in the corner of my yard like he did most of the time? I went out and called for him until it got so cold my hands and face were hurting.

Several of the other deer came in and looked at me with puzzled expressions. Sweety never came down that night. Sweety hardly ever missed a meal that I could remember. Maybe one or two nights if he was out romancing, yet even that was uncommon. The snow was deep. It was well below freezing. I couldn't sleep. I tossed and turned and cried. The next morning I hurried and put my shoes and coat on and went outside to see if Sweety was there waiting for me. No Sweety. He was nowhere in my yard. I searched again until I had to go on to work. I finally told Beth and Trish what had happened to Sweety and how he was missing. They both knew this was bad. They'd heard about Sweety for years and knew how much I loved him. They kept telling me, "Oh, he'll be back. He always comes back." I reminded myself of that over and over.

That afternoon a friend of mine walked into the office to tell us that on her way home from Gunnison a mountain lion had run out in front of her truck at around eleven that night. I did not want to hear that. I asked her where she saw the lion, and she said right in front of the Valley View Ranch. My heart sank. The ranch was Sweety's home when he wasn't with me. I couldn't keep from thinking the worst. My heart felt empty. I prayed to God, like I had done so many times before when Sweety disappeared. I also prayed to Daddy. I always felt like Daddy was listening to me when I prayed for Sweety. Even though Daddy was gone, Sweety brought him back into my life. I prayed and prayed, but yet I didn't feel Daddy could hear me. The feeling was odd, and I felt so very alone.

It felt strange not to feel anything when I prayed. I always had a warm feeling surrounding me. Sometimes I even felt like someone had touched my shoulders. I know that sounds crazy, but I felt it and now I felt nothing. I asked several people who I knew I could trust to please look for Sweety, and I showed them his picture. I called Don and told him what happened and that Sweety hadn't come in. Like everyone, Don said that he would come back. I know he knew this was pretty serious and it would tear me apart if Sweety didn't come home. Robert and I searched every night. Walking through the deep snow was hard, and it was miserable for the both of us. We didn't find Sweety, but we did find lion tracks. After the first week without Sweety I knew he was gone. I knew he would never come home again. No matter what people said to me to reassure me, I knew Sweety was gone. I knew Sweety would never leave me. He loved me too, and if I was ever sure about anything, I was sure about that. Sweety loved me as much as I loved him! The thought of never kissing that big old nose or never having him lay his big head in my lap just ripped me up. My goal now was to find his body and bring him home. I had to find Sweety!

Several people came into the office or would call me thinking they saw Sweety, but something told me that it wasn't him. Several weeks went by, and Robert and I hiked miles and miles. We were both worn out and I was half crazy. I'd heard the game warden had found a dead deer close to town and that just made me sick. I knew if he had found Sweety my chance of burying him in my yard was pretty much no chance at all. I tried to find out what the buck looked like, and after talking with Edna Mason I felt it wasn't Sweety.

On the weekends Jennifer and even Lane and Shaylee hiked, looking for Sweety and calling him. Jennifer came upon a large dead buck near a house in the Riverside area. She just knew it was Sweety; but as she came closer she realized it didn't look like Sweety's antlers. They brought the head in for me to see it, and I recognized it. It was Slick. I hadn't even realized he'd been missing. My only thought was that the night I saw Sweety and him fighting, Sweety must have killed him. Robert also found a dead buck during our searches clear down at Pete's Lake. He was surprised that he could not see any sign of it until he nearly stepped on the body. In a deep hole he had found Two Cute. All we could think of was the night we had heard shots. Someone had killed Two Cute, but they could not find him because he had fallen into that deep hole. We were saddened to find both Slick and Two Cute dead, as they were the Riverside bucks, and they were something to see – two magnificent creatures. Losing them was awful; yet we couldn't find Sweety, and I knew I would not stop searching.

One night I had a dream, and it was so vivid and so real. I could see Sweety's dead body in a deep ditch. I felt like I was right there and could see the rocks, the snow, the tree branches, and I could see Sweety clearly. I told Robert and Jennifer that morning about the dream; and when I got to work, I told Beth and Trish. The dream was like no other dream I've ever had. Now when we hiked and searched for Sweety, I looked in every drainage, every ditch, and in every hole. Robert looked too.

Weeks went by and I began to lose hope of ever finding Sweety. I talked to my sister Linda several times about everything I was going through. Linda lectured me, saying, "Sis, don't ever do this again. Don't ever fall in love with these wild animals." I knew she was right. I told her I would never do it again. Still, I'd say, "Linda could you turn your back on a small fawn that's been orphaned and walk away?" Linda said, "No, Sis," and we both agreed we wouldn't even like ourselves if we could turn away from something starving and in need of help. Our bellies were full. We weren't going without a meal. I don't know – this was such a struggle of the heart. Why did I get so involved? I didn't realize when I helped Sweety and Sly years ago that it was going to turn into years of togetherness and a friendship like no other. I felt I'd truly lost my best friend when I lost Sweety. I had never in my life spent as much time, and most of it quality time, with any of my human friends than I had with Sweety. I never went out of my way for my human friends like I had for Sweety. All he had to do was walk in the yard and he had my attention instantly. I was guilty of ignoring some of my human friends. I was never guilty of ignoring Sweety. It was crazy, but in order to put it all to rest I knew I had to find him.

The snow began disappearing and that helped Robert and I hike further in the mountains. The temperatures were warmer, but it was March. There were days when Robert and I fought over searching for Sweety. Robert was sick and tired of it. We had put hours and hours in and lots of miles. I knew he and I had other things that needed doing, rather than spending another day searching. My grandchildren needed my attention! I would watch them every Saturday afternoon and keep them at night; but Sunday was my day to hunt, and Jen would come and get them early so I could head out. Everyone understood what I was going through; although they also let me know it was too much. I realized I wasn't any good with anyone at that time. I was depressed and didn't really want to be around a lot of people. I couldn't share with many of them because so many had a bad opinion on my caring for a deer. So I kept to myself. I continued praying, even though I didn't feel I was getting listened to. I couldn't forget the dream I had. I kept reminding myself that the dream came from above and it was telling me where I had to look. The dream, I prayed, was either God's way of helping me or Daddy's way of reaching out to me, or maybe Sweety wanting me to find him. What if it was my Sweety? As I hiked, there were moments when I thought maybe he was with me. I sure couldn't share that with anyone or I'm sure the white coats would be sent to take me away. Crazy, yeah there were times as I went through all of this that I felt crazy. I'd lost so many family members I'd loved with all my heart, and yet Sweety's death was tearing me up nearly as much as losing my own sister. That was hard to explain. Cindy was my world when I was growing up. How in the world did Sweety become such a huge part of my life, and why did I allow this heartache to invade my every moment?

I painted several lion pictures. I am pretty sure a lion took Sweety's life.

Chapter 43

The Last Time, Saying Goodbye

I had days I couldn't concentrate on anything. I was so angry at myself for letting myself get this involved with an animal that could never be mine. Sweety wasn't a dog, cat, or horse. Still I thought of him as mine. The thought of not ever finding him and bringing him home was literally tearing me apart. God had to be tired of my praying and begging to him to let me find Sweety. I'd be at work, and while I would be putting out the mail, I would be quietly praying and crying. I fought the tears back every second and had to turn my head away from customers several times to avoid them seeing my tears. I think it was not really knowing what happened to Sweety that was killing me. I knew he couldn't have starved to death in one day after I saw he'd had hurt his teeth. His teeth were all that was really wrong on the last day I saw him. His foot had nearly completely healed. I knew he wouldn't live long like he was at the time, and starvation would most likely be the reason he would die. Why hadn't he come back that day his teeth had been knocked loose? I had no answers that satisfied me. Did the lion get him? Did the game warden take him? He shouldn't have died that fast? I needed answers and wasn't going to be happy until I found them. My family wasn't going to be happy until I found them. That was the worst thing that could happen. My unhappiness made everyone else miserable. I could have kicked myself. I was hurting not only myself but everyone I loved.

One afternoon Robert and I took another hike up into the mountains. We both were extremely fatigued. It was becoming exhausting, and we both were beginning to feel our searching was useless. We had hiked about two miles above our house. We had hiked this same area before, but felt we should try once more. On our way back, Robert walked the ridge of a ravine looking along the ditch as we climbed down. I just went from one place to another combing every inch so as to not miss anything. We hadn't started back for more than a minute or two when Robert yelled, "Karen I see a dead buck down close to the bottom of this ravine near the water. But Karen, I don't think it's Sweety." I yelled back at him to wait for me and not go down to it until I reached him. As I came closer to Robert he kept saying "I don't think it's Sweety." I just looked at Robert and said, "Yes, Robert, it is Sweety." He said no again, I don't think so. I said yes it is. I knew it was Sweety. I had no doubt. It was just like I saw in my dream. There was snow, there were tree branches, and down deep by the running water from the ditch lay the dead buck. I took one look and knew it was Sweety. Robert climbed down first and I followed him, trembling all the way. Neither of us said one word. Robert picked up Sweety's head and antlers, but his body was nearly completely eaten. His carcass had been shoved up under a lot of brush and leaves and looked as if whatever was eating on him had tried to hide him. Robert handed me Sweety's beautiful head, and I clung to it, holding him as tight as my arms could hold him. Oh God, it felt like a part of me was dying right then and there. Robert carried all that was left of Sweety, and we both pulled ourselves back up above the ditch onto the mountainside.

We both sat down on the ground when we reached the top. I held Sweety's head and rubbed my hands across his nose. God how I loved his wide nose! It had been partially eaten. I hated that. I squeezed his antlers. They were so beautiful, even if he had declined some. He was so beautiful and such a wonderful animal. I looked up at Robert, but when I did, Robert broke down. We both broke down. Robert said he'd miss him too, and what a great animal Sweety was. Robert said, "Karen, we're taking him home. He's going home!" I said, "It's over. We found you, Sweety." I was just bawling, my eyes were so full of tears I could hardly see to walk. I worried on my way down for fear that someone might see us and take Sweety away from me. I had heard where the Division of Wildlife could confiscate the antlers and head of a deer if they felt it was a trophy buck. Sweety was a trophy! That was the last thing I needed! How unfair that seemed. Find a small two point dead buck and probably nothing would be done, but find a deer like Sweety and I might not get to keep him. He belonged with me and no one else. He belonged in my yard, where he loved to be. It had been his home most of his life, and it was where he should be buried.

As we walked down the mountain, Robert said that he thought, by the way it all looked, that Sweety had been killed by a mountain lion. It was because of the way we had found Sweety hidden. Most other predatory animals didn't hide or bury their prey. I also felt that Sweety had been killed by a lion. Robert and I talked about which way was the best for Sweety to have died. We both agreed that getting killed by a lion was far less painful than starving to death. I couldn't have stood watching Sweety slowly die from starvation. Robert said God took him the best way possible. Sweety died quickly and didn't suffer.

Sweety was home! The minute I opened the gate and carried him in, I broke down again. I was thankful that we had made it down and no one saw us. Now we would bury Sweety. I called my daughter and told her we had found Sweety. Jennifer began crying so hard that we both couldn't talk and had to hang up the phone. I didn't call anyone else in town to let them know for fear of losing Sweety. I couldn't lose him again. I called Don and left a message on his answering machine that I had found Sweety. He was the only one I told at that time.

Robert and I picked a spot in our yard, not far from our big pine tree. It was a spot where many times I'd seen Sweety resting. Robert dug the hole and I wrapped Sweety's eaten body and beautiful head in towels and placed him down into the hole. We had a funeral. I am not sure how many mule deer have had funerals, but Sweety had one; and he might as well have had a hundred friends there bidding him farewell, as I cried enough for all of them. It was over. I wrote on my calendar "Sweety's Home, March 18, 2005."

I eventually told others about finding Sweety. It's been years, and not one day has gone by that I have not thought about Sweety. I'm ninety-nine percent sure that we have a buck in our area that is Sweety's son. He is an outstanding buck! I try not to name them anymore or get too close to them, but I gave this awesome creature the name of "Elway." I felt that was a fitting name for such a magnificent creature.

The winter before the winter when I am writing this was a horrible one. After many people in town begged to be able to feed the town's deer, they let us. Lane, Shaylee, Robert, and I all helped out. It was a great experience for my grandchildren, Robert, and me to be able to do it legally. I was thankful the

Division of Wildlife let us feed the deer and thankful that our new wildlife officer knew they needed help. Still, I believe that winter we lost a huge number of deer in the Lake City and Powderhorn areas. I've heard tales of several hundred carcasses being found. Lake City's town deer seemed to have survived, although I believe they were weakened some. Their antlers the next summer grew very odd. Many of the bucks' antlers were not at all like antlers should be. One would be tall, while the other would be short and curved; just not right. I saw a lot of broken horns. One buck that had been in the area took a drastic turn for the worse. His decline was so drastic that I think it must have been from the lack of nutrition.

Our warm season is so short, and winter is so long. It's hard for wildlife to thrive in country like ours.

I went to Tennessee this year, and while I was there I could not believe all the deer feeders in that state. I would walk into sporting goods stores, and right in the middle of the stores were huge stacks of deer food. I was told that nearly everyone fed the deer, and most fed to draw them in to be killed. Their deer, which were mostly white tail, have a lot of lush ground. I could not believe how green Tennessee was. I felt it was a crime for people to feed the white tail when God is without a doubt providing for these animals. I guess people can shoot several deer in a year down in those states. The white tail deer seem to be over- populating! Colorado, this year, will probably have to cut back on deer hunting, as we do not have enough deer to hunt after the harsh winter before. Nature though is amazing, and the deer, in time, I pray will come back; I'm sure they will.

The Riverside Bucks are nearly all history now. Grumpy is still around, and it's good to see him once in awhile. He is an old man though, and we probably won't be blessed to have him around much longer. The King is gone. There's not been another king since Sweety, not in Riverside. I miss my Sweety. I will miss him until I die. I'm sure I'll see him in heaven; I know he's there, and I hope I make it.

I've been through a lot with all of this. I know I will never put myself through this again. Was I wrong? When it all started, I believe I wasn't looked at as doing wrong. A lot changed with time. Laws changed and laws were enforced. We must respect the law. I only hope that those who make the laws will respect us too. We are only human. Sometimes our hearts are bigger than our brains. I loved Sweety and I miss Sweety. He won my heart. Was I wrong? I wonder what God's answer to my question would be? God, was I wrong?

Sweety's gravesite in my yard.

Memories I will treasure forever.

Memories of Sweety and Me Together.

Grumpy

Pedro

Squirt

Sweety

Cutler

Elway